THE
seventeen
BOOK OF YOUNG LIVING

THE
seventeen
BOOK OF YOUNG LIVING

BY *Enid A. Haupt*

EDITOR and PUBLISHER, *seventeen* MAGAZINE

Illustrated by CYNTHIA ROCKMORE

DAVID McKAY COMPANY, Inc. • NEW YORK

136.73

H29p

36137

February 1958

Manufactured in the United States of America

Van Rees Press · New York

CMT

Contents

CONTENTS

GETTING ALONG WITH BOYS

BECOMING AN ADULT

THE SEVENTEEN PARTY NOTEBOOK

Introduction

THE TEEN YEARS are an arc that stretches from the warm safety of childhood into the challenge and independence of the grown-up world. An arc that, in its slow vaulting curve, develops the rich flowering of the human soul. Nothing is new about adolescence —each generation has experienced the same phases of biological, physical, emotional, and social change. Yet everything is new about your adolescence—you are growing up *today*, learning to conform to the customs of *today*, living through the events of *today*.

Your generation of young people is not only the finest our country has ever known but also among the most blessed. For the free climate of thought in which you associate and dream permits a greater variety of observations and experiences than any previous group of teen-agers has ever known. You are taking great and good advantage of the bounty set before you and, young though you may be, you are already making your own return. With open hearts and willing hands you devote millions of hours each year to human needs through community welfare work. Millions of you are members of youth groups whose projects are vast and varied. And you have contributed richly to the national economy—nine billion dollars in earnings and allowances in 1956 alone, half of this from you, the gentler sex.

The chapters in this book are designed as keys to help you in this arc of life—to help you understand yourself, the boys and girls who are your friends, and the adults who people your world. No one but you can handle your own first encounters, but the keys for making them happy experiences are here. So, too, are the smaller but still important keys to smooth handling of the social situations that can loom as great hurdles if you are unsure of how to meet them.

I have often been asked why I so enjoy working with and for young people. There is no secret to the association. I remember vividly the moments of wonder and anguish I experienced in my youth, the hopes and dreams, the joys and frustrations. Conversing and exchanging thoughts with young adults, helping, advising, and developing young minds, give me special joy.

Writing this book has been a nostalgic experience for me. It is natural for me to associate with girls, for I am one of a family of seven sisters. Today, as women and mothers, we retain the close relationship we had in our youth. We were then and are now all of a different nature and today travel down various paths leading to individual interests. Yet fundamentally we have the same fondness and respect we exercised for one another when we lived at home together. In times of teen-life crisis, our lone brother often was called on to help solve our problems. I can only hope that the help offered in this book will measure up to the understanding and wisdom he showed us then and still does today.

In my own daughter's life, sisters were replaced with activities—sports, music, ballet, drama, arts and crafts. Today, these activities are as close to her as a family, and she uses them daily as a teacher in a preparatory school.

The writing of my book is now finished. I earnestly hope the suggestions I have offered and the experiences I have recounted will ease some of the tension attendant to the series of "firsts" that accompany adolescence. I shall feel humble and proud if I have helped to smooth away any of the blocks and hurdles disappointments can sometimes engender. If only a few are encouraged to re-examine a problem and try a fresh approach, I will be gratified; if many take a courageous, lighthearted view, I will be ever heartened.

Youth is the early springtime of woman. You have seen the reaffirmation of God each spring as the earth bursts into flower and winter-stark trees reach blossoming branches upward to the sky. Make your springtime such a one that all the seasons of your womanhood will be a radiant fulfillment of the promise you are today.

ENID A. HAUPT
Editor and Publisher
Seventeen Magazine

Getting Along
With Yourself

1. *Getting to Know You*

THE TEEN YEARS you are living now span a time when the world, all its treasures and all your future happiness, seems to be tumbling at you out of a giant cornucopia. The stars seem nearer than they may ever be again. You love more fiercely, strive harder against tough odds, accept more magnificent challenges than you ever will again in all the long life science is making possible for mankind. For this is a time of first efforts, first awareness, first experience, when the opportunity to be great, to do great things, seems almost in the hollow of your hand. It is a very big job you are tackling, even

3

with your tremendous energy and your great dreams; so, as you set out to circle the world, you need first to have an understanding of yourself. Basically, *you* are all you have to work with, so you need to know the qualities, the strengths—and the weaknesses, too—of the material at hand.

The big change   The teen years are a time of wonder-making excitement for you. They represent the beginning of your second seven-year change. (It is thought we change every seven years of our lives.) The first seven years spanned your life from babyhood to school child; suddenly you had earned a measure of independence and you became what the experts call a "middle-aged child." But still a child. Now you are at a bridging period as you part from childhood and cross over into young adulthood. It's a memorable time, one you'll never forget, for this age can't be duplicated. If you put your heart and energies into it, you can remain an attractive woman young in spirit all your life. But you can be adolescent for just seven years, and science will never find a way to duplicate this lovely April.

The teen years offer you a lavish opportunity for selecting, re-selecting, and then selecting again what you want to make of your life. Your father has probably teased your mother a hundred times about her feminine prerogative of changing her mind. Remembering this, you, as a girl, will enjoy to the brim these very separate seven years of adolescence when you have the privilege of changing your mind with greater freedom and perhaps greater approval than you will ever have again!

What's changing—you!   Change is a word that seems to be synonymous with your age. Your bone structure, which seemed nonexistent when you were three, all-existent when you were a leggy six, may have disappeared again for years under a cloak of "baby fat." (Baby fat is often closely allied to quarts of chocolate milk, lollipops, cup-

4

cakes eaten in secret, and so on.) But somehow at about twelve you start to show the first promise of the kind of body and bones you will have at sixteen. And you and your friends will be a little alarmed to find that you are all considerably taller than most of the boys you know, and your dreams of pumps with two-inch heels must be quickly discarded in favor of shoes flat as ballet slippers.

By now you know about menstruation and what it contributes to your life as a woman. You feel very grown up to understand all this—and if you're not sure you understand clearly, ask your mother, sister, or young aunt, or your family doctor, or perhaps ask your mother to get you one of the fine booklets on the subject written just for girls your age. You know that immaculate cleanliness, good diet, moderate exercise, and eight hours of sleep every night are all needed to give you a sense of well-being at this time.

What you eat and how much you eat begin to matter a good deal to you because you want to be attractive and you know that means having a bright clear skin and a nice figure. Sports are a big part of your life as you improve your skill at games, and you also look for special exercises that give you a willowy waist, easy graceful posture, and a flat middle.

Your clothes become increasingly important to you, and rightly so, because you are seeking to be an individual and your outward appearance is an indication of your personality. Your room, too, is an expression of you—the way you have fixed it, the way you keep it (neatly, I hope!), the pictures you put up, the treasures that represent memorable points in your life that are pleasurable to recall, from an aged Teddy bear to a college pennant.

Your mind is blossoming rapidly, like one of those Oriental flower shells you put in water; and you are absorbing so much knowledge, so many impressions, that sometimes you have to spend hours doing what seems to be nothing. This will be described as daydreaming (often in annoyance by grownups who are impatient to get somewhere or to get something done) , but actually you are healthily recharging your mental energy.

Your heart and your feelings are tightly strung, and your emotional response is generally a big one. You love deeply, weep abundantly, hate fiercely, enthuse beyond measure, but your feelings change as rapidly as the frames in a movie film. The great example of adolescent love was Romeo and Juliet (you remember Juliet was just fourteen) , and a favorite pastime of realists is to speculate on the lovers' feelings for each other had they lived to celebrate their silver wedding anniversary.

The subject of manners fascinates you, for you want people to like you; and a charming teacher, an older girl, or an aunt or cousin who always knows and does "the right thing" may become your ideal. Or the ideal might be an older brother or your aunt's new and glamorous young husband. And just as you are pleased by good manners, you are dismayed by bad ones—and you may find that the boys you know have quite bad ones indeed. By the time they are eighteen or so, the rough edges will be gone. Meantime you might just as well accept them for what they are—and, on the whole, what they are is disinterested in girls and the things girls are interested in—and stay friends with them by being kind, companionable, and uncritical. You will reap your reward in a few years when they *are* interested in pleasant, amiable female company.

Most of the companionship that every human needs will come in early teen age from your sisters and brothers and from girls. Many girls will want a dozen or more close friends; others will want only one or two close friends. It's your choice—a choice that you will be making all your life as your interests and the pattern of your life vary—but the important thing is to have friends and to be a good friend yourself.

Money becomes a very tangible commodity in your teens. Money means so many hours of baby-sitting, the red party dress your mother says the family just can't afford this month, the ballet lessons you want so much, the search for a summer job so you can have the ballet lessons. Money means knowing how to make your allowance do the things you want it to do. Money means putting aside a little of your allowance and a little of the money you earn so you have a fund for special things that come along.

Making the most of what you are   This is a very important key to a happy life. If you are a flaming redhead with delicate white skin, there is little future in longing to be an olive-skinned brunette. And if you are a small olive-skinned brunette, it would be difficult indeed to become a Junoesque redhead with delicate white skin! Instead of useless longing, why not accent the positive values of what you are? Rather than being embarrassed by the flaming hair—and by people nicknaming you Red or Bricktop or whatever—remember that in Ireland red hair is called queen's hair and its rare beauty is much admired. And remember the lovely lines from *Cyrano de Bergerac* when Cyrano is telling Roxane of his love:

> You know how, after looking at the sun,
> One sees red suns everywhere—so, for hours
> After the flood of sunshine that you are,
> My eyes are blinded by your burning hair! *

Surely two positive thoughts like these should make you hold proudly your head crowned with queen's hair!

And if you are a small brunette (and wish you were a tall blonde), consider this: many of the *femmes fatales* of history were little women, and more than their fair share were brunettes— Josephine, Madame de Pompadour, Ninon de Lenclos, the Duchess of Windsor!

* Edmond Rostand, *Cyrano de Bergerac*, English version by Brian Hooker (New York: Henry Holt and Company, Inc., 1924).

Every person is blessed with many assets and seemingly not so blessed with a few liabilities. More often than not, the difference between the compellingly attractive person and the one who hasn't quite got it is the way the man or woman has developed both the assets *and* the liabilities. Attractiveness and personality require the courage, determination, and honesty to face a liability squarely and try to make it into an asset. So take a good look at what you are. Take pride in the good things—whether they're a pair of limpid violet eyes, long slim legs, a stunning tennis serve, a knack of dreaming pleasant tunes by ear at the piano, the ability to get a 90 per cent average. Take a longer look at the not-so-good things, think of all you can do to improve them, and discuss ways and means with some member of your family whose advice you respect.

How do you recognize your assets? I like to think things out on paper and this is how I would go about it: I would make a list of the good things and, right beside it, a list of the bad things about:

looks
   hair
   face
   figure
   voice
   grooming

blessings
   family
   friends
   pets

talents in
   art, music, dance, dramatics

character

courage
honesty
loyalty
sincerity
reliability
kind disposition
good nature
determination
willingness to profit by mistakes

ability in

each school subject
sports
cooking
keeping house
sewing and mending
handcrafts
earning money

interest and activity in

school organizations
school clubs
church organizations
community groups

social skills

bridge, canasta, and such
entertaining
letter writing
talking easily to other young people and adults

If you have some trusted older person you can talk freely to—a big sister, an aunt, for example—you might show the list to her. Chances are you've underrated a lot of your assets and chances are you have quite a few you didn't know you had!

The threshold of life All this adds up to the exciting fact that you are on the threshold of life, with the opportunity for everything that's good in front of you. There is nothing you can't achieve. You live in a wonderful land of opportunity where people of humble background have developed their God-given talents and assets into great, fine lives: Abraham Lincoln, Irving Berlin, Marian Anderson. Whether you become a great doctor, teacher, or humanitarian is not necessarily important. But you must *be somebody*. Not anybody or nobody. Make the most of what you are, so that you will stand for something that you can be deeply proud of. One of the characteristics of the French race is this pride each person takes in what he is and what he stands for—the woman who makes *perfect* omelettes, the man who is the *best* tailor, and the girl who is the *best* milliner in town, the young matron who raises *exquisite* roses.

It is idle to dream away your days *wishing* to be somebody or to do great things. Contrary to the song, wishing won't make it so. The meaning of idle, according to Webster, is to waste. If you do something constructive, you'll be happy. If you do nothing constructive, you will be unhappy and you will have wasted all the bright promise of your youth.

So, before discussing all the ways you can set about becoming somebody, let us first try to understand what makes you tick.

2. *What Makes You Tick?*

TRYING to figure out what makes a girl in her teens tick is a little like trying to understand and put together one of those do-it-yourself kaleidoscope kits. And it's certainly just as colorful! But the brightly colored emotional patterns of your life during adolescence actually have a structure of meaning that can be described very simply. You have an emotional framework to your life that is composed of basic human needs and drives, plus—and this is the element that baffles so many young people and their parents—*plus* some special and transient emotions that color your teen years. How you use these drives and this overgenerous serving of vivid emotions will strongly determine the quality of the adult personality that you are building now.

In the life of every animal and human being there are three basic needs; these are: hunger, shelter, and sex. Most babies born today find, immediately upon birth, the satisfaction of their hunger and their need for shelter. And, with the first touch of a human hand, they feel the comfort and protection that is a baby's first emotional re-action and a portion of the total part of sex in human life. If you've been lucky enough to have newborn kittens or puppies in your house, you've probably observed that they have these same satisfactions in common with man—the mother feeds them upon birth, they snuggle into her fur for protection and shelter, and she licks them affection-ately. And I'm sure you've watched kittens often and seen how, after they're fed, they roll and purr in contentment. But, unlike kittens or puppies, you are part of the human race. You can think, and these basic needs interreact with your conscious and unconscious thoughts. These thoughts affect the three basic emotions of love, hate, and fear. And here again, unlike kittens or puppies, these basic emotions all interact with your conscious thoughts. This kaleidoscope of inter-reactions of a human's conscious thoughts, basic needs, and basic emotions is called the unconscious. By the time you reach your teen years, you have built two kaleidoscopic patterns—one of your *conscious* emotions, memories, and habits; the other of your *unconscious* emotions, memories, and habits. The important years of thirteen through nineteen form the framework of the personality you will build out of these two kaleidoscopic patterns.

And because you are striving in your teens to build the finest personality you possibly can, you seem to have an extra set of very special emotions charged with the nervous energy that is charac-teristic of any person engaged in a big, almost overwhelmingly im-portant job. You think big, your reactions are big—there is absolutely nothing small about the dreams of a girl in her teens!

Recognizing these special teen emotions will help you understand the dynamic quality of your feelings and the speed with which you

12

can switch from love to hate, from enthusiasm to scorn, from elation to despair.

You ask WHY I once heard a successful businessman say that the most valuable man in any company is the one who asks "WHY?" And that quality of restless discontent with existing rules and with authority is certainly the sign of a young, creative, thinking mind. It can be described in one word as rebellion, and it is the emotion that causes the most trouble for teen-agers at home, at school, and abroad. Rebel you will, rebel you must. But it is necessary for you to be responsible about this emotion. There is constructive rebellion —it builds something. A better solution to a problem; a better understanding with your family or your teachers; a better deal for you, your friends, and the other people involved in the subject under discussion. And, unhappily, there is destructive rebellion—it destroys. It may destroy your family's or your teachers' confidence in you, it may lose a privilege for you and perhaps your friends, and you will know you didn't do your best.

Here is a typical situation and two ways it could be handled:

The case in point: Your parents say no dates during the week. You think this is cruelly unfair because many of the other girls are allowed to have at least one early date during the week, your marks in school are good, you never (almost never) slip up on doing your room and any other household chores you've agreed to do, you are kind and good to your parents and your little brother and sister, and if you have to be a stay-at-home you may lose your friends and especially the boy you like the best.

Your parents have said that's that and they don't want to hear any more discussion of the subject.

You handle the situation destructively: You tell your family you are going to Jean's house to study or to work on some social or civic

13

project. Actually, Jean has invited one other girl, two boys, and, at your request, your beau. It is ingenuous to think that your disobeying will not get back to your family. Among the many consequences you have to take are your parents' hurt surprise at your deception, their probable loss of confidence in you, possibly their forbidding you to see Jean and your beau again. You have flouted authority and gotten your own way—but the price is high.

Or—you handle the situation constructively: You take a poll of all your friends whose mothers are friends of your mother. You find out just how many are allowed one or more dates during the week. If the tally is two or three girls out of ten, forget the whole thing. But if it is five or more out of ten, you are in a fair bargaining position. One that calls for public relations in the home.

You wait till your mother is relaxed and willing to talk to you (not just as she is rushing out to the supermarket or the hairdresser; not when she is putting the last touches on a dinner party for your father's college classmate who has been away for the last eight years). You ask her if she would be willing to consider a solution to a problem that's bothering you. You tell her that you realize that she and your father are right about your not going out on dates during the week but that Jean and the four or five other girls (whose mothers are friends of your mother) *are* allowed at least one mid-week date. Explain that your friends are important to you and that you would like to keep up with them—but that your parents' approval is more important. Suggest that, since both are anxious to have you learn to be a good cook, perhaps they would be willing to let you ask your beau and one other couple for an early dinner one night a week. You would plan it, market for it, cook it, and clean up after it—and you would promise that the supper party would be over by nine o'clock. And if your marks took a skid, you would give up the supper party till they got back up to your usual good average.

14

In other words, whether your problem is at home or at school, try to offer the authorities a solution to the problem that will be acceptable to them. Work *through* existing channels—rather than against them or around them. The Orientals are famed for their wise and gently polite ways of dealing with other people, and the principle of saving face is a very important one to them. If you are lucky in having toddler-age cousins or nieces and nephews, you may have heard the youngster's parents wheedle him out of a touchy temper-triggering situation by offering him what they call a face-saving alternative. As he is about to storm over having Grandpa's heirloom watch removed from him (and Grandpa should have known better!) the child's parent says quickly, "Stevie, did you hear the fire engine going past?" or "Stevie, find your blue ball and I'll throw it to you." Stevie has something tangible to think about and to do, Grandpa's watch is saved, no one has wept or been cross.

And parents and school authorities sometimes need face-saving solutions offered in the same spirit. Not to outfox them but to make it easier for them to retreat from a previous, very positive position.

Idols—near and far   Everybody has idols. The name may be different depending on your age or sex. The long parade of idols in a girl's life goes somewhat like this:

age	idol that's near	idol that's far
two	wonderful Daddy	easy—you're just beginning to live
five	kindergarten teacher	cowboy star or TV emcee
nine	probably no one—you hunt in packs at this age	the current singing sensation

age	idol that's near	idol that's far
eleven	an attractive teacher	a baseball star
thirteen	an older girl	a movie star, a singer, a ballerina — depending on your interests
fifteen	any member of the first, second, or fifth squad of the football team	a movie star (male, this age), a minister, a TV star, a sports star
seventeen	the boy next door	could still be the boy next door

People of all ages have idols, whether they describe them as idols, crushes, ideals, or heroes. Your father may have the President of the United States and the third baseman on his favorite ball team for his. Your mother probably has your father for hers. Your young uncle may think the president of his company is his ideal of what he would like to be himself. People admire others for many reasons—their looks, character, achievements, personality, popularity; and because admiring someone who is somebody usually raises your own standards of excellence and gives you a greater goal to head for, your current idol is probably helping, not hindering, you.

The kind of idol to watch out for, to surrender with all possible speed, is the one who stands for something that is not fine, excellent, and good. You can't always tell immediately that an idol has feet of clay. When you do, find another better fitted to be your ideal.

A boy or girl who, like Satan, tempts you to do things you feel are wrong—or that would be wrong in the eyes of your family, school, and friends—can cause you only heartache. Your standards of ethics and morals are pretty well set before you are of teen age. You realize there is little reward in doing things that will make you unhappy or ashamed. You know that no one else can make you do anything.

It hurts to find that an idol is far from ideal. Even the most renowned genius will make errors in judgment of others. As in the case of the great composer, Ludwig van Beethoven. His worship of Napoleon Bonaparte was legendary. He looked upon Napoleon as one of the greatest liberals of his day; and to honor him, Beethoven inscribed the name of the then First Consul of France on the title page of the famous *Eroica Symphony*. Only a few months later, Beethoven's hero had shown himself to be greedy for power, and the shocked and outraged composer, seeing his idol had feet of clay, struck Napoleon's name from his masterpiece.

The sting of disappointment The main reason a disappointment hurts so keenly at your age is a rather touching one—you haven't had a great many of them and it is very hard to get a disappointment in perspective. Why should this happen to you, you wail. Well, it should because it is very necessary in life to be able to handle disappointments courageously, without making those near to you suffer your misery unduly. Of course you will need to talk out the sting of a disappointment; it may be one that will cause you regret all your life. But in St. Augustine's classically beautiful book, *The City of God*, there is a line that says, "As in the same fire chaff burneth and gold shineth." Through meeting disappointments well, the human soul is refined so that the good and golden part shines.

You can't win them all is a remark beloved by the sports broadcasters, and if many people in the world let disappointment or defeat smother their ambitions and crush their spirits, we would be missing a great many of the blessings we take for granted. Marie Curie might not have discovered radium; the Wright brothers might have agreed that man could never fly; Alexander Fleming would have given up the notion of deriving a magnificent medicine—penicillin—from bread mold; and Lucy Stone would have settled back with her embroidery rather than struggling to win equal voting privileges and equal rights for the women of the United States. *None of these great people achieved success until they had faced and conquered many disappointments and seeming defeats.*

If you lost out on becoming president of your class or of your club, if you didn't make the honor society at school, if your family couldn't swing the cost of the trip to the lake, if the boy you like best has asked another girl to the dance—these are disappointments that hurt and stun. The best thing you can do is to take part wholeheartedly in other interests that will keep you too busy to be unhappy. Concentrate on developing your mind and your talents, learning new skills, new sports—you will very likely discover so much new happiness that you will marvel at the intensity of your past misery.

Who does she think she is? One of the bad ways to face disappointment is to be envious of the girl who got the boy or won the election, or of your cousins who are going to the lake. The dictionaries have many unattractive descriptions of the word envy—"to regard anything with grudging, longing eyes," "to show malice or ill will." One of the splendid things about participating in sports is that, pretty generally, the people you play with will see to it that you behave well when you or your team lose. If you are not "sportsmanlike," chances are you won't have anyone to play with. No one wants to spend an hour on the tennis courts with a girl who may be grumpy or weepy if she loses. No one wants to play golf with someone who grouses all around the course when she's off her game. No one will take you sailing if you insist on being the skipper every time.

So, if you are disappointed at losing, try to take pleasure in the happiness of your friend who did win. Tell her she played beautifully, that she outplayed you at every turn. (Very bad form it is to indicate that *you* weren't playing your usual good game!) You can learn a great deal from those who are better than you—they are in a very real sense your teachers if you are willing to learn. If your friend who won the tennis game has a good backhand or a superb serve, ask her to teach you how to improve yours. Or, if your beau is a fine dancer and you are only fair, he probably will get a pleasant sense of accomplishment—and a nice boost to his masculine pride—if you ask him to help you become a good dancing partner.

If your cousins are taking a trip and you can't, make them less unhappy about your disappointment by asking them to write and tell you the news and to send you snapshots when they can—and write cheery letters to them about the new interests you've developed.

Jealousy and heartbreak are two strong emotions you may suffer when you fall in love, and you know this just by listening to the titles of the ten top records on any hit parade. Both can be very poignant to you, both can make you feel helpless and ill-treated because the one you love can be partly responsible for your jealousy and your heartbreak. With purpose and determination you can mend the mistakes you make but there's not much positive action you can take about another's mistakes. The best thing you can do is find someone else. Not necessarily a better someone else—never minimize the qualities of someone you've loved—but someone with whom you can build a finer, worthier relationship. We'll talk more about heartbreak in the section about getting along with boys.

You didn't do your best This is an unhappy feeling that can plague you in your teen years. Your standards are so high, you want to accomplish so much, that you are dismayed and chagrined when you've used what turns out to be poor judgment. There's one comfort for you to know: whether yours was a big or a little mistake, you are neither the first nor the last person to make mistakes of all sizes. Instead of being ashamed, you should say to yourself, "I could have done it better." That's positive. After all, usually you are the only person who knows you've omitted part of a story or made a mistake. The only real tragedy from an error is not learning from it. Many mistakes come from carelessness, forgetfulness, stubbornness, and so on. These you can understand and explain. But when you've used the best judgment you had available at the moment and you've still made a big blunder, don't brood about it. You'll meet the situation better next time. And like the fliers who get into another plane as soon as possible after a crash, plan not only to meet the situation you flubbed the very next time it comes up—but why not try to create an opportunity to go through the same experience soon again, and see if you can't deal with it more effectively? I'm sure you will! It's a great waste of time to fear a situation; if, like the fliers, you do something positive, you'll be too busy to be afraid.

A way to measure success is if one is right more often than wrong. But no one has a perfect score.

Here's a test that quizzes both your personal traits and the way you actually behave in everyday life. There are two columns for you to check—Yes and No. You can discover your personality-building level below.

How High Is Your Personality?

1. If your parents forbid weeknight dates, would you make them anyway and pretend you were visiting a friend?   Yes—— No——

2. Would you charge things to your parents' accounts without permission?   Yes—— No——

3. Would you try to get extra baby-sitting jobs in order to have enough money for a special dress or record album? Yes—— No——

4. If the boy you like best asked your best friend to the spring dance, would you still be her friend? Yes—— No——

5. If your team lost the basketball game, would you claim the other team cheated? Yes—— No——

6. If you muffed most of your lines in the school play, would you go to the party afterward? Yes—— No——

7. If you ran for a class office and lost, would you run again the next year? Yes—— No——

8. If you were visiting a friend for the weekend, would you go out with a boy your parents disapproved? Yes—— No——

9. If your school banned sororities or secret societies, would you try to get a group to present a club program—a French circle, a bridge-canasta club, a fashion group—that the school would sponsor? Yes—— No——

10. Would you invite friends in, without permission, when you are baby-sitting? Yes—— No——

21

If you had two Yes answers, you have built your personality as high as a ranch house. If you said Yes four times, you've gotten high as a split-level house. If you said Yes five or six times, you've reached the skyscraper level and you have my warm congratulations!

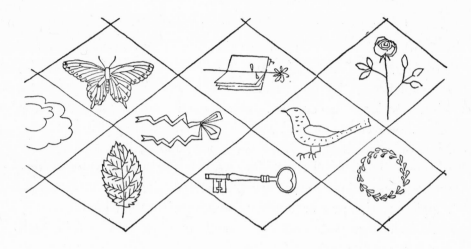

3. *Take the Matter of Your Mind*

HOW HIGH you build your personality will depend largely on the energy and creativeness you apply to this fascinating job of construction. Only the young really have the energy to meet the tremendous challenge of youth, so let us agree that the first requirement is taken care of! But about the second, creativeness. Creativeness is the courage to try new things, the eager willingness to learn, a questioning habit of mind that says: Can it be better, more useful, more beautiful—and what can I do to make it better?

Of course, talent has its place in the creation of anything worthy, but attaining the dignity of years is not a necessary attribute. You've seen many beautiful paintings by young children; Mozart played the piano superbly at the age of seven; Ruggiero Ricci was a re-

23

nowned violinist in his early teens; Patrice Munsel was a great singer and Susan Strasberg a great actress before reaching their seventeenth birthdays. The contribution that years make to creativeness is the accumulation of learning, the chance to practice and perfect, the wisdom to judge. Talent and creativeness are not one and the same thing, however. If you are blessed with great talent, that is fortunate. Most of us are blessed with creativeness, and perhaps that is more fortunate. Think of what a tedious world it would be if everyone were great—a great singer, great artist, great ballerina—with no average, happily creative people to enjoy and appreciate their talent!

So, as a major part of your personality building, you learn to reach out for new interests that give color and texture to your mind, achieving the richness of a mosaic by the time you complete the arc from childhood to adulthood.

This richness of mind will affect all the undertakings of your life—your work, play, the interweaving of family and friends, all social and civic activities—making each hour of the day have extra meaning for you. You will always have something to do. Better, you will always have a dream to cherish.

Take the matter of your mind In school you have learned many basic mental skills by now. You read and write, you can handle figures, you have fairly well oriented yourself in relation to country and history. Most of you realize that, once you've mastered the basic skills, the art of thinking and of knowing how to find the information you need is far more valuable than a prodigious memory for facts and dates, mathematical formulas, and so on. If by now you know how to take any topic—say it's herbs—and go to the library and research it, you are well on your way to using your mind creatively to reach out for new interests. (By researching herbs, for example, you can learn fascinating things about the cuisine and customs of people in the Latin countries, the Near East, and around the world;

24

you can learn about the use of herbs as medicine in medieval Europe, the housekeeping problems of Elizabethan England where rush-strewn floors were sprinkled with herbs and where ladies carried herb bouquets to counteract the lack of the vacuum cleaners, detergents, chlorophyll sprays, hygiene, and sanitation we know today; you'll learn about indoor and outdoor herb gardens and about the perfume business today. Herbs are certainly not a subject of earth-shaking importance, but they give a stimulating example of how an interest in one minor topic can widen your world, make the history and plays of the past closer to you, and even give you a new hobby.)

Serendipity is a wonderful omnibus word that means looking for one thing and finding other things as well. It's a very good mental skill to develop although, admittedly, it can slow you down when you're in a hurry. I have discovered that it's almost impossible for me to look up one word in a dictionary without being lured into reading descriptions of quite a few others. It is, however, a good way to learn, especially when you apply it to a broader scale of activity than dealing with a dictionary. Farther along in this chapter I will list the steps for doing an intelligent research job—with a little serendipity, too!—so you will know some of the steps for putting your mind to work at building the personality you want.

But now, just like a woman, I have to criticize serendipity for a moment. If you let your interests wander over too great a variety of subjects—rather than concentrating on a few—you will be a jack of all trades, master of none. That is why you need to set goals for yourself, with deadlines, and when the date of the deadline arrives, you need to see how near you've come to your goal and, if you've missed it, why.

What your mind can do for you   It's been the custom in New York City over many decades for the mayor to present important visitors with the key to the city. Your mind, properly nurtured and encouraged, can be your key to the whole world. It can unlock a lifetime of pleasure and satisfaction in reading, art, music, ballet, space travel or world travel, teaching or playing an instrument, nursing or medical research, being a housewife or a dress designer (or both!). No matter what your family's present financial, social, or civic position may be, you are an heiress, a princess in the inheritance of your mind, that most obedient servant.

Think of some of the services it can perform for you. It can help you achieve the goal you set for yourself. By developing your own mind you learn to appreciate others and the things they accomplish. It helps you to make money—and today one out of three girls in their teens has a part-time job; this year teen-age girls received from earnings and allowances nearly five billion dollars.

If you give your mind a chance to unfold, you will be a happy person, blessed with interests and activities all your life. An intelligent seeking mind helps you win friends and keep them, helps you to achieve and maintain a good marriage and a successful family life, shows you the way to being a better, more skillful mother. And a more useful citizen.

And another point that can be very satisfying: Among the fruits of all these services that your mind can do is the pride and pleasure your family—and your future family—will take in the things you accomplish.

How to put your mind to work   Here are four steps for getting full measure out of researching a subject that interests you:

1. Decide on the subject.
2. Read everything you can borrow from family, friends, library, and special groups interested in the subject.
3. "Ride the hobby"—talk about it to everybody and you'll discover fascinating side lights to the subject that interests you. (Here

serendipity is at work again.) You will also find two other values to this hobby riding: boys and girls, adults will take on new charm, character, and personality when you find a kindred soul who is interested in your hobby or who has something to contribute to your pursuit of your hobby. And secondly, you will, early in adolescence, master the art of conversation on matters other than gossip about people and parties.

4. If you can—depending on where you live and the condition of your grades at school—take a special course in your hobby. There are night classes and extension classes in many schools. The Girl Scouts, YWCA, 4-H groups, women's clubs, all have programs you can join. Or ask your parents, teachers, church, or doctor. Or call your newspaper for information, the local hospitals or the Red Cross, the Chamber of Commerce, and so on.

How do you study? Whether it's your schoolwork or your hobby, study is certainly in order. What does the word mean? Webster says it is the setting of mind or thoughts upon a subject to be learned or investigated, the application of the mind to books, art, or any subject for the purpose of acquiring knowledge.

I often hear about young people and adults who are so wrapped up in a subject that they can study under any conditions—in a crowd of people or in a room with the radio or television at top pitch—but that isn't a very healthy way to go about studying and enjoying a subject. These are the things I do when I set my mind upon a subject. First, I choose a quiet room where I hope I won't be disturbed. At school this is no problem but often, in a big family, you have to do a certain amount of preplanning to ensure quiet. Suppose you share your room with your sister—and your sister is a gay, bubbling, talkative girl—and your room is the only available spot for study. What I would do, if I were you, is to say you need a time for study when you won't be disturbed. Try to make it at the same time every day, perhaps when you know your sister has a favorite TV show she could watch. Hang a PLEASE DON'T DISTURB sign on the door (like the ones in hotels) *after* you have announced your "study hall" system to the family and asked for their co-operation.

My next move in studying is to be fairly sure that all the equipment I will need is at hand *before* I settle down to work. This would include books, notebooks, pencils, pen, typewriter, paper, erasers, glasses if you wear them. I also add whatever things I need to pamper myself or give me an extra lift of energy over a complicated problem—these may include carrot sticks, raisins, a few crisp salted crackers, a pitcher of lemonade or water or a thermos of hot tea—the idea here being to close the escape hatch of discovering things that will take me away from the work at hand. Many of the authors and copywriters I've worked with over the years have told me of the dodges they use before they can actually discipline themselves to write the first line of the story: getting a glass of water, sharpening all the pencils, putting a new ribbon in the typewriter, writing a long-overdue letter, and so on! So my advice is to be alert to your own temptation to procrastinate, if that is your nature.

After I clear a working space for myself, I sit down and review exactly what is to be done in the time allotted. And more often than not, it helps me to make a list so that the most important thing is not left until the end, either to be put off till tomorrow or to be done with less than the attention it deserves.

What do you put your mind to?   In New England they say crisply, "You can do anything you want to if you put your mind to it." So now, at the point when you are busy taking stock of yourself, you might want to set up a list of goals in the various activities of your world:

SCHOOL

your goal should be to get the most information out of each class, paying heed to your teachers' suggestions for outside reading, field trips, extra study classes, related radio and television programs, records you can borrow from the library. By doing this, each class will be more interesting to you, you will retain what you learn because you have helped bring the learning to life—and you will undoubtedly get better grades. No training period is better than your high-school days, for these school years are a plan in miniature for the pattern of your adult life.

SCHOOL ACTIVITIES

you will need to weigh carefully the activities you participate in. It would be fun to be the president of your class if that is what you want—but only one person can achieve that office, and if you do not, you might turn your sights to another phase of school activities. You can gain as much respect as a participant of a group as you can as a leader. You may be another type of person entirely and prefer an individual activity. If this is the case, by using the same amount of time and energy you could join a ballet class or take up modern dancing or one of the many activities in the field of fine arts. There are practical measures, too, which can be most rewarding, such as learning typing and shorthand with others in your school. Activities such as these not only give you excellent qualifications for turning in better and more efficient schoolwork, but prepare you for a job when you have finished your education.

SPORTS

here, too, you need to see your goal clearly. Group and team sports are a challenge and give a great sense of camaraderie in

29

victory or in loss. If, however, you do not qualify for a team, indulge in sports, anyway, if only for exercise and fun. To perfect your ability in a sport will add immeasurably to your social life. Ability to join in the fun at the local tennis courts or to be a companion on the golf course adds a dimension to your personality. Sailing, swimming, and skating are excellent ways to improve your grace and figure. There is always the chance that you may surprise yourself and become a skillful sportswoman as a by-product of pursuing a sport for fun. You could then possibly qualify for a team. The least you will have accrued, however, are the benefits of health and many enjoyable hours.

CLUB ACTIVITIES

the wish to be with your special friends is never stronger than when you are deciding on what group activities to join. At this moment of decision your individuality will be more in focus, for what group you choose and what the organizations accomplish reflect directly back to you as a person.

you may want to make your mark in a large organization such as the Girl Scouts, Campfire Girls, 4-H, Hi-Y, and the like. You may lean to groups that are occupied for the most part with social activities and pastimes such as bridge, canasta, etc. You may have the personality that needs both types of expression. If you have the time, it is good to balance your interests, combining community projects and the purely social.

if your personal goals take second place to friendship, try to interest a few of your friends in your preferences and to combine companionship with accomplishment of purpose. But it is possible to pursue your ambitions and have friends in other activities. In this instance your time must be carefully budgeted.

30

CHURCH WORK

most churches have youth groups that serve both to educate the young members of the church in their religion and to form strong ties of fellowship through picnics, suppers, evening dances, and various church societies. This is an important part of the foundation you are building for your future.

COMMUNITY WORK

much of the community work you will contribute to does not require a definite amount of work each week since it centers around specialized drives. However, when you plan your activities, see what time you can devote to settlement-house work, hospital work, children's playground activities, or well-baby clinics. Perhaps you might discover that some of your friends—both boys and girls—would rather forego some of the club life and join in on interesting community projects where you all would gain a heart-warming sense of accomplishment.

EARNING MONEY

this is a fairly universal teen activity, with one out of every three teen-age girls being a part-time earner. Whatever you and your family decide you may do to earn money, whether it's helping at the supermarket, working in a dress shop, baby-sitting, or typing envelopes, try to study the people you work for and with. You will soon learn what makes a person a good employee and the satisfaction that comes from feeling you have turned in the best job you could. Ask your father to help you work out a plan for saving a part of each dollar you earn, and with his help, decide what you are saving it for. Perhaps to buy a guitar, or sterling silver, or some special item of clothing you would not otherwise have. Or it might be set aside toward the tuition for college or graduate school.

31

Budget your time as you do your money. To get full value from it you must study yourself. There are no set rules for using time, for we are all creatures of a different nature. Some of us are quick learners and some slow learners. Neither title reflects on your intelligence. The first important goal to set up in learning about yourself is how much time *you* require to accomplish a task well.

Curiosity of mind, to me, is the richest endowment a person can possess. To develop in the art of conversation and to broaden your own capacity as a person, use your eyes really to see the wonders of nature and man. Go to the museums, go to the libraries, go to visit churches of religions other than yours, go to your local historical sites. Wherever you go, look, look, look. Try to study the developments in a particular phase of art or literature that has a particular interest for you. Study the dance—modern or classic—study music, modern or classic, but study something that falls outside the range of your daily life. This is the way to develop a hobby. Once you know a subject fairly well, you automatically find yourself wanting to know not only that particular subject but those allied to it. Thus your pattern grows and develops as you do. And when this happens, you are no longer just a person—you are a *personality*.

The wonderful world of books Have you ever thought of the wonderful places that lie between the covers of a book? I have had the greatest experiences. I have dined vicariously with royalty and shared bread with peasants. I've known heroes and heroines, knaves and navigators, poets and princesses in high towers, attended chariot races in ancient Rome, arrived in the New World with Columbus, and wept quietly with sorrowful soldiers on the blood-drenched battlefields of the Civil War.

I have cried when the great composer, Wagner, was hissed out of the opera house in Paris, and I have speculated what life will be like in 1984. From all these exciting peaks and pinnacles, I have ob-

32

served and visited lands and people near and far. Their conversation and their customs I find fascinating far beyond imagination's richest dreams. To learn the history, arts, and crafts of people of different cultures is to weave a tapestry that forms a mosaic pattern from which you can reset stones and designs as simple or as complicated as you choose. Here is a list of enjoyable and entertaining books which are available at libraries and bookstores. You might discover a wonderful new world in any one of them:

A. *Music*

AMERICAN BALLADS AND FOLK SONGS, by John A. and Alan Lomax. New York: The Macmillan Company.

BUILDING YOUR RECORD LIBRARY, by Roy Hoopes, Jr. New York: McGraw-Hill Book Company, 1956.

THE ENCYCLOPEDIA OF JAZZ, by Leonard Feather. New York: Horizon Press, Inc.

THE ENCYCLOPEDIA YEARBOOK OF JAZZ, by Leonard Feather. New York: Horizon Press, Inc.

FAMOUS NEGRO MUSIC MAKERS, by Langston Hughes. New York: Dodd, Mead and Company.

FIRESIDE BOOK OF FOLK SONGS, Margaret Bradford Boni, editor. New York: Simon and Schuster, Inc.

THE FIRST BOOK OF JAZZ, by Langston Hughes. New York: Franklin Watts, Inc.

MEN AND MELODIES, by Leonard A. Paris. New York: Thomas Y. Crowell Company.

MY LORD, WHAT A MORNING, by Marian Anderson. New York: The Viking Press, Inc.

PEOPLE OF NOTE, by Laurence McKinney. New York: E. P. Dutton and Company, Inc.

A PICTORIAL HISTORY OF JAZZ, by Orrin, Keepnews, and Bill Grauer, Jr. New York: Crown Publishers, Inc.

THE STORY OF ARTURO TOSCANINI, by David Ewen. New York: Henry Holt and Company, Inc.

THE STORY OF GEORGE GERSHWIN, by David Ewen. New York: Henry Holt and Company, Inc.

THE STORY OF IRVING BERLIN, by David Ewen. New York: Henry Holt and Company, Inc.

THE STORY OF JAZZ, by Marshall W. Stearns. New York: Oxford University Press, Inc., 1956.
   Clear analysis of jazz as blending of European and West African music.

SYMPHONY CONDUCTORS OF THE U.S.A., by Hope Stoddard. New York: Thomas Y. Crowell Company.

THIS IS AN ORCHESTRA, by Elsa A. Posell. Boston: Houghton Mifflin Company.

THE WORLD OF OPERA, by Robert Lawrence. New York: Thomas Nelson and Sons, 1956.

YEHUDI MENUHIN, by Robert Magidoff. New York: Doubleday and Company, Inc.

B. *Art*

A NEW WORLD HISTORY OF ART, by Sheldon Cheney. New York: The Viking Press, Inc., 1956.
   Painting, sculpture, architecture, and the minor arts through the ages.

A PRIMER OF MODERN ART, by Sheldon Cheney. New York: Liveright Publishing Corporation.

PULL UP AN EASEL, by Norman Garbo. New York: A. S. Barnes and Company.

THE RAINBOW BOOK OF ART, by Thomas Craven. Cleveland: The World Publishing Company, 1956.
   From cave paintings to current masters—for the beginner.

WATER COLOR, GOUACHE AND CASEIN PAINTING, by Adolf Dehn. New York: Thomas Y. Crowell Company.

34

C. *Dance*

ALICIA MARKOVA, by Anton Dolin. New York: Thomas Nelson and Sons.

AT THE BALLET: A GUIDE TO ENJOYMENT, by Irving Deakin. New York: Thomas Nelson and Sons, 1956.

BALLET TEACHER, by Lee Wyndham. New York: Julian Messner, Inc., 1956.

THE BORZOI BOOK OF MODERN DANCE, by Margaret Lloyd. New York: Alfred A. Knopf, Inc.

THE DANCE IN AMERICA, by Walter Terry. New York: Harper and Brothers.
A history for a serious student.

DANCE TO THE PIPER, by Agnes de Mille. New York: Grosset and Dunlap.

FAMOUS BALLET DANCERS, by Jane T. McConnell. New York: Thomas Y. Crowell Company.

FAMOUS DANCERS, by Jane Muir. New York: Dodd, Mead and Company, 1956.

GIRL'S BOOK OF BALLET, A. H. Frank, editor. New York: Roy Publishers, 1956.

HOW TO BECOME A GOOD DANCER, by Arthur Murray. New York: Simon and Schuster, Inc.

MODERN DANCE: TECHNIQUES AND TEACHING, by Gertrude Schurr and R. D. Yocom. New York: The Ronald Press Company.

MOIRA SHEARER, by Pigeon Crowle. New York: Pitman Publishing Corporation.

PARTNERS ALL—PLACES ALL!, by Miriam H. Kirkell. New York: E. P. Dutton and Company, Inc.

STAR PERFORMANCE, by Walter Terry. New York: Doubleday and Company, Inc.

D. *Books and plays*

ABE LINCOLN IN ILLINOIS, by Robert E. Sherwood. New York: Charles Scribner's Sons.

CAESAR AND CLEOPATRA, by George Bernard Shaw. New York: Dodd, Mead and Company.

THE CAINE MUTINY COURT MARTIAL, by Herman Wouk. New York: Doubleday and Company.

COMPLETE WORKS OF WILLIAM SHAKESPEARE, edited by G. L. Kittredge. Boston: Ginn and Company.
> Includes *Romeo and Juliet*.

CURTAIN GOING UP!, by Gladys Malvern. New York: Julian Messner, Inc.
> The story of Katharine Cornell.

CYRANO DE BERGERAC, by Edmond Rostand, edited by Brian Hooker. New York: Henry Holt and Company, Inc.

THE IMPORTANCE OF BEING EARNEST, by Oscar Wilde. New York: British Book Centre.

I REMEMBER MAMA, by John Van Druten. New York: Harcourt, Brace and Company.

MEMORIES, by Ethel Barrymore. New York: Harper and Brothers.

MR. PICKWICK, by Stanley Young. New York: Random House.

OUR TOWN, by Thornton Wilder. New York: Coward-McCann, Inc.

STORIES FROM SHAKESPEARE, by Marchette Chute. Cleveland: World Publishing Company, 1956.

SAINT JOAN, by George Bernard Shaw. New York: Dodd, Mead and Company.

TEEN THEATER, by Edwin Gross and Nathalie Gross. New York: McGraw-Hill Book Company.

E. *Things to do*

AN INVITATION TO CHESS, by Irving Chernev and Kenneth Harkness. New York: Simon and Schuster, Inc.

LAST OF THE CURLEWS, by Fred Bodsworth. New York: Dodd, Mead and Company.
> The humanized account of a bird which annually flew a round trip from Patagonia to the Arctic Circle.

36

MAKE YOUR OWN: TEEN-AGE CLOTHES, ACCESSORIES AND GIFTS, by Kay Hardy. New York: Funk and Wagnalls Company, 1956.

MY HOBBY IS BIRD WATCHING, by Mary Pettit. New York: Hart Publishing Company.

NATURE'S WAYS, by Roy Chapman Andrews. New York: Crown Publishers, Inc.

PLANTS: A GUIDE TO HOBBIES, by Herbert Spencer Zim. New York: Harcourt, Brace and Company.

WINDOW IN THE SEA, by Ralph Nading Hill. New York: Rinehart and Company, Inc., 1956.

F. *Things to dream about*

ACROSS THE SPACE FRONTIER, by Cornelius Ryan. New York: The Viking Press.

ANGEL OF THE BATTLEFIELD, by Ishbel Ross. New York: Harper and Brothers, 1956.
Life of Clara Barton of the Red Cross.

DOCTOR KATE, ANGEL ON SNOWSHOES, by Adele Comandini. New York: Rinehart and Company, Inc., 1956.

THE EXPLORATION OF MARS, by Willy Ley and Wernher von Braun. New York: The Viking Press, 1956.

THE FIRST WOMAN DOCTOR, by Rachel Baker. New York: Julian Messner, Inc.

GREAT ADVENTURES IN SCIENCE, by Helen Wright and Samuel Rapport. New York: Harper and Brothers, 1956.

THE LIFE I'VE LED, by Babe Didrikson Zaharias. New York: A. S. Barnes and Company, 1955.

PROFILES IN COURAGE, by Senator Robert F. Kennedy. New York: Harper and Brothers, 1956.

SCALPEL, by Agatha Young. New York: Random House, 1956.

SEVEN WONDERS OF THE WORLD, by Lowell Thomas. New York: Hanover House, 1956.

4. *You're Pretty As You Can Be*

AS YOU are growing up, you begin to realize that the outer you is a reflection by which all other persons measure the inner you. And as you build your own sense of responsibility toward yourself, you are heightening the standards by which you want to be measured by others. You're learning to be proud of being somebody, and therefore your outward appearance is beginning to reflect this inner pride you have in being part of your world.

Attractiveness, the well-being of mind and body, is an attitude, just like every other habit of life. Your development along the arc toward adulthood reflects your increasing ability to have pride in the well-being and attractiveness of your body. During these young years, grooming will occupy a good measure of your time, for your pride demands that you be as nearly perfect in outward appearance as you have time and energy to make yourself.

You have known, just as I have, women whose features could never be made more regular by make-up tricks. Inwardly, however, each has developed so much charm and warmth that if a casual acquaintance remarks, "She's nice but she's certainly no beauty," you have to think twice about your attractive friend's appearance. She's beautiful to you!

Handsomeness in men or women, boys or girls, is a gift from God. Beauty is what God wanted every human being to develop within himself. And it can be developed by you as you grow in understanding your own inner charm and as you learn to project your charm—and your interest in others—to others.

And just like all areas of human endeavor, the standards you set for your outward appearance will grow in scope and meaning as you begin to realize your own ideals of the kind of woman you want to be.

Suppose we think about the standards you should be meeting now. . . .

Beauty from the inside out

DIET

let's discuss diet first. You watch your food for two reasons: health and good looks. You'll find it simpler to pass up the chocolate malted today than to wash away acne tomorrow. You will be hungry. Make no mistake about your appetite disappearing; it won't. All you can do about it is to satisfy your craving for food in the right way. You need food—sometimes as many as five meals a day—and you will for several years, for you are changing and your physical and emotional changes eat up energy. Nature makes you hungry, and you will need to supply your body with the right foods in the right amounts to keep your energy at top level.

girls with a flawless complexion may have to diet to control weight while their slender sisters must diet for skin problems. The best and simplest overweight diet is not to eliminate foods but to cut portions in half. Should the past eating problems have been extreme in nature, no one knows more than the overly indulged just how she must balance the calories. An average maintenance diet for an active teen-ager is 2400 calories. A healthy diet, but one to lose about two pounds a week, varies between 1500 and 1800 calories. The foundations for any diet should include the foods that are the basis for good health:

DAILY FOOD GUIDE

1. Four or more glasses of milk each day—fresh, evaporated mixed with an equal portion of water, or nonfat dry. Cheese and ice cream are important substitutes.
2. Two or more servings daily of protein—meat, poultry, fish, or eggs. Dry beans, peas, and nuts may be occasional substitutes.
3. Two or more servings of fresh, frozen, or canned vegetables; one of potatoes.
4. Two or more servings of fresh, frozen, or canned fruit. One must be of citrus fruit or tomato.
5. At each meal, one or more servings of enriched or whole-grain bread, cereal, or flour products.
6. In moderation and according to need, fats and sweets. Butter or margarine at every meal.

to figure out how much you should eat each day—based on the Daily Food Guide—you should first arm yourself with a pocket calorie guide (they're sold at most stationery stores). If your weight is fine, you can eat up to 2400 calories of the basic daily foods.

if you're overweight, stick to the Daily Food Guide—but trim the calories to 1500 to 1800 a day to trim you.

proper eating habits are a state of mind, and, just as your emotional habits toward many things were developed in early youth, your emotions about eating were formed then, too. When you were a youngster, a treat was often a lollipop, cake, or a sweet drink. During your teens—when you may be emotionally upset by the events of the moment—you feel like babying yourself, and what could be more comforting than foods you've come to look on as rewards?

then, too, in your family, your mother may get great pleasure out of being a fine cook and she probably has always smiled with delight when you were able to eat everything she put before you. So, if you should watch your diet—because of overweight or because of a skin problem—you'll need to enlist your mother's aid to have her smile approvingly when you pass up her beautifully baked pies and cakes. Eating less and eating non-fattening foods, however, can give you a great feeling of accomplishment as your waistline slims down and your body firms into attractive lines.

EXERCISE

what does exercise do to keep you trim? Here is a table gleaned from the Harvard University School of Public Health; it shows you the number of calories burned in a half hour's exercise.

Walking (moderately fast)	94
Roller Skating	102
Ice Skating	102
Dancing	105
Tennis	149
Basketball	149
Field Hockey	149
Swimming	217

while exercise rarely takes off poundage, it does firm your body and thus reduces by inches rather than by pounds. Competitive sports and activities outdoors bring a healthy glow to your skin. I like to take long walks in the country observing nature's infinite beauty, or a walk in the city where man's miracles can be seen on every hand. I find it does wonders to relieve worries and puts my problems in proper perspective. As you walk you might learn to think of the Quaker rhyme: thy chest out, thy stomach in, thy head up, thy chin in—and let your arms swing freely at your side. Along with walking, other forms of outdoor exercise such as swimming, tennis, badminton, ping-pong—and in winter, ice skating, field hockey, and paddle tennis—give your body a glorious feeling of health. Have you learned a new sport this year? Why not take up one in earnest tomorrow?

poor weather will sometimes keep you from exercising outdoors, so along with fresh-air and outdoor activity, it is wise to develop a routine of stretching and bending exercises. These need be done only a few minutes a day, but give excellent results. The stretch I like best is to walk around the room picking imaginary apples from a tree. Try always to get the highest ones, and your waistline will never boast a bulge. For the bending, my favorite is to stand with feet apart, toes turned outward. Touch the left hand first in front, then in back, of the right foot without bending your knees; alternate the action for the

right hand and left foot. As a consequence of the pull, it narrows out your hips and waist. And these two exercises done faithfully each day can eliminate your measurement problems. Try doing these to the tune of your favorite records, and you'll find the exercise period speeding by.

The Daily Dozen Check List

Here's a good check list for you to copy on a slate and put by your mirror. Attach a piece of chalk to the slate and every day tick off your accomplishments. After a while, the daily standards you want to meet will become so much of a habit you won't need the reminder.

- *Take a shower or bath* that includes an allover scrub with a heavily lathered washcloth. Be sure you soap ears and neck (well into your hairline) and use a hand brush on fingernails and toenails and on rough skin of elbows and heels. Plenty of rinsing with clear water is another must.

- *Use a deodorant* or anti-perspirant.
- *Dust* on bath powder.
- *Clean nails*—toes and fingers.
- *Smooth* on hand lotion.
- *Wear clean* underclothes, socks, or stockings.
- *Brush your teeth* after breakfast and dinner; after lunch if you can.
- *Clean your face* at least twice a day, using the method that's best for your skin.

43

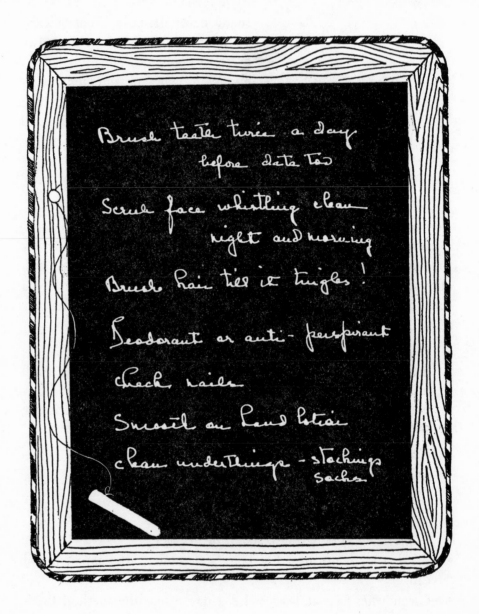

- *Brush your hair.*
- *Check your bag* to be sure you have facial tissues (fold them into a clean handkerchief), lipstick, compact, pocket comb, tiny clothesbrush. If your face requires a noontime scrub, you might add a disposable washcloth.
- Eat all six types of basic foods.
- *Get outdoors* for a walk or some kind of exercise for an hour.

Beauty that's at least skin-deep

YOUR SKIN

during your teens is likely to be lovely if you keep it immaculately clean and if you are careful to eat the foods listed in the Daily Food Guide. Habits of skin care are of the essence. After your routine is set to meet your personal needs, it is of the utmost importance that the program be carried out. For the regularity and thoroughness of the care you give are as needful as the regular feeding and cleansing of your body. While a clear glowing skin comes from the inside out, you may experience bouts of surface trouble because of glandular changes which pour forth oily secretions that clog the pores. To keep this annoyance under control, wash your face twice a day with warm water and soap (try one of the new ones that contain a bacteria-killing agent) spread generously on a clean washcloth; scrub well into the hairline, where skin eruptions frequently begin, and be sure to rinse thoroughly.

If you have continued skin eruptions or an eruption that is more than a plain blackhead or common pimple, ask your doctor's advice; he is the best judge of how to treat infection.

MAKE-UP

is a delicate subject for teen-agers. I believe firmly that a sparkling eye, a natural smile are still the best cosmetics ever

45

invented—and they were not invented by man. If make-up is not for you as yet, be glad that nature has endowed you with the natural beauty of youth. And if you are of an age, in your community, to use make-up, remember that its purpose is to enhance your natural good looks. A good rule to follow is to use a little less than you think you need. This is one time when you really might rely on your mother's opinion because she wants to see you at your prettiest, and on this matter she is probably a much better judge than your mirror!

For daytime, you'll probably want to use a colorless protective base lotion that will not only help your face powder last without retouching but will also act as a safety barrier to keep powder on, not in, your skin. You may prefer loose powder to a pressed powder, but in either case, make your first purchase at a good store where a trained salesperson will guide you to the right shade for your skin coloring. And do invest in a supply of throwaway puffs or cotton squares so you can use a clean one every day; this will go a long way toward keeping your skin clean and healthy.

At your age, a light lipstick is probably the wise choice, and you will want a small wardrobe of colors to compliment the colors of your dresses and sweaters: a clear red, a pink-red, and a golden pink or coral. A lipstick brush is a help in achieving a neat lip line, and you will produce a nicer look if you blot off excess lipstick with a clean tissue. Here's an excellent way to give a blush to your cheeks: after blotting your lipstick with tissue to remove the excess, touch the cheeks lightly with the used tissue. This gives just enough color to the cheeks and guarantees a color that blends with your lipstick.

For evening parties, you may want a make-up base with color to use under your powder; whether you choose a liquid, cream, or cake, use it sparingly and follow the maker's instructions. Eye

46

make-up requires both skill and secrecy to be attractive; the mildest amount of eye shadow can be smoothed from the center of your eyelid out and up to your eyebrow. Mascara should be applied with a fairly dry brush to give a feathery look and keep lashes from clumping together. If you are the proud owner of an eyelash curler, use it before putting on mascara.

Do be sure you remove make-up thoroughly once the party's over. Liquid cleansing lotion, or cleansing cream and skin lotion, or plenty of warm water and a sudsy washcloth will do the trick.

YOUR HAIR

will never be more lustrous and manageable than during your teens, so take advantage of this particular springtime beauty blessing by shampooing faithfully (this will also protect your complexion) and brushing vigorously with a clean hairbrush. A good beauty habit is to shampoo your brush and comb when you wash your hair; you can use a bit of shampoo in warm water and then rinse well.

And the same advice goes for hair styles as in make-up—the simpler the better, with your healthy shining hair the keynote, rather than an elaborate style.

A home permanent is often a help in achieving the young pretty look you want; and this is an easy skill to learn now—and one you'll use all your life. Before giving yourself a home permanent, get a really good haircut; be sure to tell the hairdresser that you plan to give yourself a permanent and describe the way you want it to look. Taking along a clipping from a magazine may make it easier for both of you.

YOUR TEETH

need plenty of brushing, too, after each meal. Ask your dentist how he wants you to brush them and what kind of brush, dentifrice, and mouthwash he thinks are best for you. You should have at least two toothbrushes, so you will always have a dry one to use. And if you can't clean your teeth after lunch, remember that dentists look on an apple or a raw carrot as "nature's toothbrush," so you might plan your lunch to include one of these.

If money is a problem, do remember that most hospitals have dental clinics both for regular visits that include cleaning and filling and also for straightening teeth that need orthodontia for good looks or good health.

FINGERNAILS AND TOENAILS

deserve a weekly treatment, including use of cuticle remover, nail trimming (toenails straight across, please), oiling and pampering with hand lotion. If you use polish, you'll need to wash nails clean of oil and cuticle remover and put the hand lotion on *after* your polish is thoroughly dry. I like to see the clear or rosy-tinted polish used in school and the brighter shades reserved for dress-up occasions. Remember, clear polish is more attractive than badly applied or chipped bright polish.

The use of a deodorant is a lifetime habit that is good to form right now. Deodorants come in liquid, stick, and cream form; and some stop perspiration as well as bacteria-producing odors. The ones that stop perspiration are called anti-perspirants.

You will want to remove underarm hair and perhaps hair on your legs, and there are a number of ways to go about this. You might invest in a safety razor (a major female crime is to borrow your father's or your brother's—and if you must on, say, a trip, be sure to put in a fresh blade after using it) and a cream or lotion to soften the hair before shaving. Follow the instructions on the preparation you use. There are also electric shavers for the ladies now; these come in pretty pastel colors and shave both

48

leg and underarm hair. Or you can use a depilatory, following the instructions on that package. For facial hair that gives a dark shadow there are bleaches available. Test your skin for sensitivity before you use a bleach or a depilatory on your face. Never, never use a razor. If you are convinced that unsightly hair on your face is a cause for concern, ask your doctor about electrolysis—but it is a long, expensive, rather painful process, and I do not recommend it for most girls your age.

FRAGRANCE

a whiff of fragrance goes with being a girl, and you will want to choose a light airy perfume or cologne that makes you feel fresh and attractive. But please remember to use a whiff—your perfume should never sandbag your public. Sachets to put with your underthings are pleasant, and so are the new spray sachets to use on lingerie, on bed linens, in your closet.

YOUR VOICE—TRUE OR FALSE NOTE?

one of the best keys you own for opening doors to new friendships and new opportunities is your speaking voice. It mirrors the kind of person you are, indicates your background and all that you have done to build a well-rounded, well-read personality. In *King Lear*, Shakespeare gave a perfect description of a feminine voice. He said, "Her voice was ever soft, gentle, and low, an excellent thing in woman." And that is much more pleasant to contemplate than some of the voices you've probably heard this very day—including the one that sounded like chalk screeching across a blackboard, or the mousy colorless one you couldn't quite hear, or the loud rough one that made you keep stepping back from its unlucky owner.

The next time you're at the movies or watching television, close your eyes for a minute and listen to the actors and the way they use their voices like instruments in a great orchestra. Your voice can be like theirs, too, conveying shades of affection, sympathy, interest, pleasure.

Do you know what your voice sounds like? It's probably quite different from what you imagine and the most noticeable difference, I think, is in the pitch. Your voice sounds much lower to you than to anyone else, and that's a good thing to remember because, when you realize yours is getting a touch high and shrill, you can be fairly sure that it's raucous as a siren to others.

There are many ways that are often suggested to hear yourself as others hear you—including listening to your voice as you cup your hands and push your ears forward to make a sound box. Or listening to it as you stand in the deep end of an empty swimming pool and talk (I have never found this to be a particularly easy method!).

But the best way I know is to make a recording of your voice. Many places, particularly railroad terminals, have booths where you can cut a record for about twenty-five cents, and often you will find record shops or radio stations that have this service for a moderately higher price. Voice teachers in many schools include a recording as part of their course, so you might arrange to record your voice at your school.

It's a very simple procedure: At a given signal, you talk into the microphone, using your normal speaking voice. You can ad-lib, read a passage from a newspaper or book, or, if one of your friends is interested, you might talk to each other or read parts from a play. Then you can listen to the record at home to study the tone and warmth of your voice and to see if you have any speech habits that need improving. It would be a good idea to cut another record after about six months to see how much you've improved.

A very good investment for you to make would be a pronouncing dictionary. Keep it by your bed or on your desk and browse through it every day, pronouncing the words out loud until you say them easily and comfortably. If you're not sure of how to use a pronouncing dictionary and interpret the phonetic sounds, ask your English teacher to help you.

Pretty, pleasant speech requires making separate and distinct sounds for the many vowels in the English language. Here is a list you might practice:

ā	as in	ale, whale, bale
â	as in	care, fare, bare
ă	as in	cat, mat, sat
ä	as in	arm, farm, harm
a	as in	ask, bask, task
ē	as in	eve, each, eager
ĕ	as in	end, mend, tend
ea̅	as in	early, earnest, earth
ī	as in	ice, mice, nice
ĭ	as in	ill, spill, mill
ō	as in	old, mold, fold
ô	as in	orb, absorb, corn
ŏ	as in	odd, clod, sod
oi	as in	oil, foil, boil
o̅o̅	as in	food, mood, soon
ŏŏ	as in	wood, good, book
ou	as in	house, mouse, out
ū	as in	use, fuse, muse
û	as in	urn, turn, burn
ŭ	as in	up, sup, cuff

Other things you can do to develop your voice include reading your lessons aloud in your room and listening to the pitch of your voice. Can you make a dull passage come alive? Can you underplay the emotion of an impassioned speech?—this is a trick great actors use to give richer meaning to their lines. Do you slur some words or does each syllable get the recognition it deserves? And—do you really open your mouth when you talk so that your voice comes out instead of being smothered?

A child is a wonderful sounding board for both the quality of your voice and the way you speak or read. Next time you baby-sit for a small child, read to him and watch his reaction to the story. Does he realize there was a question asked? He'll usually try to answer it if you read well. Is he eager because danger lies ahead, is he happy when the people in the story are happy? A child responds to the warmth, excitement, or pleasure in your voice; so if you fail to get his response and to hold his attention, you can know that you haven't given the storytelling all you have.

You'll have plenty of opportunity for public speaking—in class, at school and club meetings, and so on. It's a disastrous experience—and one I remember well—to stand up to speak and feel your face and voice are absolutely frozen. Here's a simple set of exercises I learned as a teen-ager that I still use to limber up my vocal cords before I speak in public; perhaps they will help you. . . .

Anti-Freeze Prescription

Repeat these words until you find your facial
and vocal muscles are completely relaxed:

THESE   THEM   THEY   THAT   THOU

My Fair Lady is a delightful musical based on Bernard Shaw's famous play, *Pygmalion*. The story's theme is that a girl might be beautiful, winsome, and charming; but without the speech and voice to project that womanliness, her life would be poor and drab. Shaw's

52

transformation of a street waif into a lady who could properly pronounce "The rain in Spain falls mainly on the plain" with full authority has led to one of the great musicals of our time that teaches us, very pleasantly, how golden a key one's voice and speech can be.

I've called this chapter "You're Pretty As You Can Be" and there is one last thought I want to add on the subject of outward beauty: Whatever you are outside reflects the beauty of soul you carry within you. No matter how classic your features may or may not be, it is the inner you that will determine whether people think you are really as pretty as you can be.

5. *Buttons and Bows*

SOME GIRLS have an innate instinct about how to dress well. They walk and act with a sense of sureness because they know their appearance is commanding. If you haven't developed this flair yet, there are tricks that will help you style yourself in a becoming fashion. See if these don't show you the way.

The first rule of being well dressed is to be suitably dressed for the occasion. Confidence in your appearance is an enormous personality plus. If you *know* you are at your best, you feel free to be completely interested in the people around you (and being interested in others makes you interesting to them).

Study yourself and experiment with ways to improve your appearance. Consider the total impression you give when you enter a room. When a truly well-dressed woman comes toward you, you never notice her dress or hair or adornments individually, only the general effect she creates.

Develop your personal color chart! Go to a store which carries fabrics by the yard and ask for help in selecting becoming shades. Hold colors up to your face. Do they compliment your skin tones or not? A fair-skinned brunette, for example, looks fabulous in yellow, while a brunette with darker skin cannot wear yellow so successfully. So a good rule for choosing colors is to key them not from your hair, but rather from your skin tones and your eyes. I mention eyes, for in my life I have known dozens of women with blue and green eyes who have accentuated this feature by wearing complementary and matching shades. If occasionally they strayed from their basic shades they used them in accessories.

Study what type you are Be honest and analytical about your good points and the ones you wish to camouflage. With the expert advice you read in magazines and newspapers you can guide yourself easily. Try to develop little habits that are individual to you—use new ways to complement your clothes by placing a pin or flower at your waistline or on your shoulder. Make short white gloves a part of your fashion personality. A feminine trick is to tuck a small chiffon handkerchief in a pocket or pull it through a belt. Pearls worn under a collar and showing only in front make the collar stand up becomingly and reveal your imaginative self. The unexpected little note of individuality is your personal fashion signature.

Your figure determines your silhouette. If you have an average figure, your choice of dress styles is wide-open. But if you do not, study yourself objectively in a long mirror to learn your proportions. Measurements tell you whether a sheath skirt or a full skirt will be best for you. If you have a long waistline, emphasize it for a fluid look. A neat midriff aided by a waist cincher enhances a short-waisted figure. This type of figure is often flattered by blouses and dirndl skirts. Pretty shoulders should be accentuated whenever possible with off-the-shoulder necklines with either a shoulder trim or a puffed sleeve.

- *If you're tall,* try to be as supple and graceful as a slender young tree—don't stoop over or slump! Lower your heel heights so you will walk fluidly rather than aggressively. Stay away from elongating styles such as vertical stripes. Wear your hair down in a page boy, tied in a chignon—any way except high on your head. Never choose a hat with a high crown, even though it may be the current fashion.

- *If you are small*—be petite—make it an asset. Don't try to be tall by wearing overly high heels. Everything from head to toe should be in balance. Height itself makes no one attractive; consequently, lack of it is no disadvantage. Your proportions are the secret. Be sure your accessories are in balance for your size.

- *If you're Junoesque* or maybe a touch plump, choose neutral or dark colors. Remember the robin has a red breast while the elephant is clothed in dark gray. Not that queen-size girls are either like elephants or should wear only gray, but nature's color schemes can teach us much. And dark colors tend to diminish weight.

- *If you are very slender,* use little jackets, full skirts, high necklines and round collars to frame your face. A tiny waist is wonderful if you can make it a feature. Stay away from anything that

56

gives a skinny look, such as a long-sleeved tight sweater or a starkly plain dark sheath dress.

Remember the old song, "Buttons and Bows"? It spelled femininity and that word spells charm. Femininity itself is a big word. It incorporates every desirable trait of the female—gentleness, allure, immaculateness, and individuality. It provokes the male to a protective sense and brings out the best male traits—responsibility, courage, leadership, and guidance. So much for femininity. For charm there is the best of all possible quotes, "that indefinable something that, if you have it, you don't need to have anything else, and if you don't have it, it doesn't much matter what else you do have."

Shop carefully   A shopping trip is an investment of your time, your energy, your talent, and your money; so a little preplanning before you set out will certainly help you make a more worth-while investment.

It helps to have an ideal (one who has a good measure of your attributes) to keep in mind as a shopping standard, a girl or woman whose taste you admire; ask yourself as you shop, "Would she wear this—or *this?*" When buying clothing, don't just buy something you love if you've no need for it. The same goes for bargains. They are extravagances if they are not usable.

Consider your goal first, in shopping. That's easy—you want to be suitably and becomingly dressed for the various occasions of your life. That means you will need to think of the many activities you engage in and of the ones that occupy most of your time. When you set out to shop, make a list of the probable occasions on which you will wear what you plan to buy.

If most of your time is spent at school, at outdoor sports, and your dates are mostly to go square dancing and sports events, you are not in the market for the pretty taffeta skirts, velvet camisole tops, organdy blouses that might be your choice if you were more involved in informal home parties, formal dances, theaters, and restaurants. You'll get more mileage out of your wardrobe if your choice runs to cardigan and pull-over sweaters, corduroys, tweeds, flannels, and cottons; then, if an unexpected informal party comes along, you can tuck the sweater inside a full skirt, add a glamorous belt, some good-looking pearl or gold jewelry, wear plain pumps, and feel very well dressed indeed. (A pleasant combination here would be a delft-blue Orlon or cashmere pull-over and a full blue-and-gray plaid flannel or tweed skirt—or a black pull-over and a red plaid skirt—or a gray pull-over and a gray flannel skirt.) You will learn this way that it is much easier on your budget to *dress up* simple clothes than it is to *dress down* the fancier ones.

Another secret of fashion success is to take your time. Don't spend your precious dollars fast. Shop alone or with a member of your family or a friend whose taste you admire. Listen to the advice of the expert who might be waiting on you. If you don't agree with her judgment, ask if the buyer in the department will help you. Explain the occasion for which you are shopping (or the places you will wear your purchase). When she sees that you are serious, she will help you to the best of her ability. She knows that if you look as well as possible, your friends will want to patronize her shop or department, too, so don't hesitate to ask for wise counsel.

And speaking of your clothes budget, I think you will find that the conservative, classic styles and colors will give you longer wear and more continuing satisfaction. And that the transitional cottons, mixtures of cotton and man-made fibers, will give you year-round use of the clothes you buy; many of these new combinations are almost impossible to distinguish from expensive silks and tweeds, yet they are washable, cool in summer, and warm in winter.

Another way of getting extensive use out of a limited budget is to look for basic items that serve many purposes. The navy-blue dress that you can wear to school or to a summer job or on a date—wearing a red-and-white striped scarf and a flower for the first two activities; a pink flower, scarf, and gloves for a date. Or a basic red coat that looks well in the daytime and is gay for evening. Never choose a loose, hip-length coat if you can have only one coat in your wardrobe; a full-length coat of a simple style will go with everything, even full skirts, which toppers war with.

Much the same kind of thinking should affect the shoes you buy. Plain black-patent pumps are the most practical of all heeled shoes. They need little care except to check that heels are not run over. They go well with dresses, suits, or skirt and shirts. Another version of this idea would be buying plain red-kid pumps for both winter dances and to wear with summer dresses. The classic kind of shoe—and the most becoming to all—is the medium-heel pump with closed back and heel. Then, of course, you'll want flats, walking shoes, shoes for any sports you are devoted to.

A good test of clothing is to simulate the activity it is intended for before you buy. To be sure the dance dress moves comfortably with you, take a few turns around the dressing room; sit down to check how the neckline appears when you relax your shoulders and to find out how the sheath skirt looks (be sure you won't have to yank it down over your knees every time you sit); swing an imaginary tennis racket or golf club when you try on the tennis or golf dress or skirt.

Never go on a date of importance without a complete dress rehearsal, including accessories. You never know whether a long string of pearls or beads looks right or one that is shortened to choker length (shorteners can be obtained at most jewelry counters and are merely glamourized clasp pins that permit you to adjust long necklaces to any length). Also, try your bag for size and your glove length and heel height. Some skirt lengths and widths give a better over-all effect with different heel heights. For example, a wedge-heel shoe is excellent with a pleated skirt but never with a sheath dress, while a sheath sport skirt and a wedge-heel flat is a splendid choice. So you see, this is a personal testing program. There are no hard and fast rules; developing fashion know-how for yourself takes time and study. But it has happy rewards and is an asset that will benefit you all your life. While styles may change, if you have arrived at your own good basic styling, you will follow only the trends that fall into the range of fashion that is becoming to you as an individual—you will develop your *own* fashion signature.

To be orderly, you can be lazy It seems to me that just about everyone has how-to suggestions of all kinds, but the ones that have the most value to me are the ones that deal with how to be lazy. Now, like the Stephen Potter *Gamesmanship*, *One-upmanship*, and *Lifemanship* books, being lazy takes some very positive preplanning.

Early in life I learned that one way for me to have enough time to be thoroughly lazy was to *put things away*. There are no problems, when you are pressed for time, if you know where everything is. You also avoid criticism from orderly parents, sisters, or even husbands. An orderly room gives you a sense of leisure, an atmosphere in which to relax and reflect, to create or read or daydream. Put clothing away soon after it is removed and you never have to face the dull chore of straightening your drawers and closets; they are always in order, automatically.

- *Closet care*. Study the cover-ups. Closets and shelves can be filled today with wonderful aids to tidiness. There are delightfully covered dress bags, hat and sweater boxes that boast a clear plastic opening panel. In this way, you know where each item is and you never have to ransack the closet to find the garment you want.
- *Shoes* in boxes, labeled, will not collect dust over winter or summer months when they are not in use. If you brush them

60

before you put them away—and better still, if you put shoe trees or a heavy wad of tissue paper in to keep them in shape—you have reduced the upkeep on your shoe wardrobe to quite a minimum.

- *Handbags* should be stuffed with tissue paper to retain shape and, ideally, should be stored in a drawer or box during the months when they are not in use.

- *Stockings, gloves, handkerchiefs* have a long prime of life when you organize their lives in quilted cases or boxes that prevent unnecessary snags, tears, and rumpling.

- Hangers are of major importance in any woman's closet. Plump padded ones—notched plastic ones—now, new foam-rubber ones —keep dresses from slipping to the floor. There are special, inexpensive, "omnibus" hangers that hold six or more blouses or skirts or shorts; these are real space savers. Other pleasantries in the closet are belt hangers and petticoat hangers, and plastic-covered hanging "shelves" in which to store your purses.

- *Tissue paper* can save you hours of maintenance as far as your wardrobe goes. Fold sheets of tissue between the folds of your sweaters to keep them from creasing. Do the same with slips, scarves, silk stoles, and nightgowns that are wrinkle-prone. Crumple tissue in sleeves that tend to wrinkle while hanging in your closet; in hats to hold their shape.

- *If you regularly wax* handbags and shoes, it can save you a good deal of effort. The new liquid-cream waxes build up a patina of shine so that all you need do, after a few waxings, is buff up the gloss, even after a soaking in the rain.

- *There are many extras* to taking special care of your clothes. Watch the tricks your mother has developed and read magazines for word on new aids. A pleasant device, too, is to promote an air of fragrance about your bureau—and you have a choice of sachets, sachet paint for your bureau drawers, sachet spray for your lingerie, and—truly!—perfumed rice.

Being well dressed and well groomed requires a very delicate sense of balance. It is not an important enough matter to absorb your whole life, and yet, if you fail to devote adequate attention to the details of being a very female person, you will never be quite the woman you might be. In the hurly-burly of contemporary living, we tend to lose track of some of the values of the past. I often like to read some of the books and plays of the Gay Nineties to recapture the iridescent sense of femininity that pervaded everything written about the heroines of that era. I am reminded by them that streamlining and speed aren't everything. Gracious ways and attitudes are still of the essence.

Looking well and pleasing others is, if we are honest, based on the desire to be pleasing in the sight of those we love: family, friends, and particularly the men in our lives, fathers, beaux, husbands. And that is probably the most pertinent of all advice in choosing clothes. If the most important man in your life doesn't like your new purchase, better think twice before you keep it.

6. *Your Room—*
Heavenly Haven

AS YOUR personality grows you will want your own room to reflect these new developments. Just as you style yourself in clothes, you will want your surroundings to reflect your personality. Decorating a bedroom or a home allows a display that is truly creative. It is often only after long speculation that you can decide your choices, for in this *you* make a statement! And your first decoration of the space allotted to you—to call your own—holds all the challenge of a first real home.

The prime decision is the type of atmosphere you want. Do you see yourself in sleek modern lines or in a canopied bed with ruffled curtains? Will you have the starkly simple and bold patterns of modern-design fabrics or the flowery patterns descended from the traditional? Do you respond to soft pastel shades or vibrant colors? Will this be your choice to make or do you share a room with a sister whose taste may be just the opposite of yours? Should the latter be the case, the best solution is, of course, careful planning by both of you. And even the combination of modern and traditional concepts can be chosen so that there is perfect harmony. Of course, a neutral decision on the fabrics would have to be reached. In this case a solid-color fabric pleasing to both would be the best choice. By careful study of your needs and allotments, any kind of room can be successfully organized. If you both study in the room, adequate space must be held for two desks. If one prefers a phonograph and the other a portable TV, a compromise is certainly needed even though the budget may allow for both. Agreements will have to be made on the occasions and times for use of each instrument. Plan beforehand with each other when you want guests in to visit. Remember—the room belongs to both of you. Foot lockers or storage space must also be very carefully planned for a room for two.

You're probably going to mix periods of furniture—whether you share a room with a sister who wants contemporary design while you like Regency or whether, like most of us, you have some pieces of furniture, acquire a few others from your family, and are able to buy a few more. Most people of taste, and most decorators, no longer feel it is essential to have all the furniture of one period to have a well-decorated room. That is fine for museums!

To have a room that is harmonious to the eye and in good taste, there are two useful keys that will help you:

1. Formal furniture of all periods mixes well, as does informal design of all periods.
2. When you choose a piece of furniture, consider the other pieces it must go with—do the lines harmonize with your other furni-

ture? Is the new piece essentially simple, or delicate and ornate; and how will these design qualities tie in with what you have? Your eye can quickly be trained to recognize relationships in design if you cultivate it by studying books and magazines which give you good visual information about furniture and decorating.

Color is your great opportunity. It carries an enormous impact; and beautiful, flattering colors can be yours at little cost. The mixing and blending of shades and contrasts can be as imaginative as you are. But if you have a monochromatic eye and are soothed by a soft beige-and-white combination, use it. You can add a few bright-colored small pillows to give a wonderful accent, should you choose. Even the rich verdant green of the leaves on a small plant will emphasize the soothing over-all cool impression a beige-and-white room will give. Or perhaps you want a year-round sunny atmosphere. Then call on yellow and white with touches of green—this combination comes right from nature's own spring garden.

How do you choose a color scheme? The colors you choose to wear and to decorate your room are all part of your personality, so it's wise to remember this when you start choosing colors and fabrics for your room. If your choice in clothes runs to beige, brown, and touches of orange, be wary of decorating your room in the pretty pink-and-soft-green color scheme that intrigued you in your favorite magazine. You might be a great deal happier in a beige-and-white room with touches of citrus tones. Or if you wear greens and reds, the delicate feminine room with pink, blue, and beige chintz and ruffled white curtains might charm you for a few weeks and suddenly bore you with its blandness. So it might be a good idea for you to open your closet door and see what colors predominate; then open the drawers where you keep your sweaters and scarves. And *then* start planning the colors of your room, based on what the artists call "your palette." (As you study great paintings you will find that each

65

artist has his own palette—the colors he puts on the thin sheet of board he holds to mix the tints and shades he will use in a painting. Rembrandt's palette was essentially rich browns, reds, and yellows; Van Gogh's, sunny dry yellows, orange, yellow-greens, and gold; El Greco's, mystic sea greens, gray blues, putty tones, and somber grays and blacks.)

People respond emotionally to color, too. On a rainy dull day, a bright-yellow room brings the feeling of warmth and sunshine. Blue and green are cool and restful to the spirits and to the eye. Pink and rose make a woman feel feminine and bring a more personal atmosphere. White, red, violet, dark-green leaf tones have a more dramatic effect.

Whatever your choice of furnishings and color, there are some basic things you will want to do to make your room the haven it should be. Here are some of them:

- Put a night table with a pretty lamp by your bed and place a few of your best-loved books on it.

- Make sure you have a good reading light. If you share your room with a sister, there are tiny spotlights that provide you with good light but will let her sleep.

- Keep visible in your room some of the things you have loved all your life—a Teddy bear, a battered hand puppet, a souvenir from the first football game you went to, a Valentine, one of those silly hats that dance bands give out, the ribbon from your first corsage. These are your life, to quote a popular TV program, and you need and want this sense of continuity. Later, when you are married, you will paste endless snapshots into a photograph album (probably with captions—I know I did!) and you will pepper your house and your parents' houses with pictures of your children. But now your delight and continuity are the arc from your childhood into adolescence on the way to maturity. It is all yours to enjoy.

If you cannot completely redecorate your room, you can achieve a new atmosphere by using room brighteners. Here are some you might try:

1. Cover part of a wall with pegboard, painted to match your walls if the room is small or to match one of the colors if your room is large. Use it to hold invitations, snapshots, theater programs, souvenirs from dances, ball games, and other treasures.

2. Ask your father or brother to help you construct a simple plant stand in front of your window. A good kind to have is one that has shelves like drawers—deep enough so you can set your plants in gravel which will hold moisture to keep the plants healthy.

3. If your room has gay chintz slip covers and draperies, use the same chintz for ruffled lamp shades but cover them with an over-flounce of white organdy—very pretty with the light shining through.

4. If you have a fine doll collection, work out some special shelves—those metal strips that hold brackets are good—to display each size of doll in your collection.

5. Cover one wall with blackboard paint—it comes in a pretty shade of soft green—and get your friends to work out a mural in colored chalk. Easy to wash off and do again when you want a change of scene.

6. Work out a gallery of your family, friends, favorites on TV, the movies, and recordings. Perhaps you could make a big frame to hold burlap, to which you could pin the pictures. Or get a real bulletin board. Or a sheet of Beaverboard which you could paint.

7. If your room is simply decorated, indulge in one piece of madness. If you have a painted chest of drawers or a painted chair, cover it with butterfly decalcomanias.

8. Get travel posters, or theater and ballet posters, to put on your

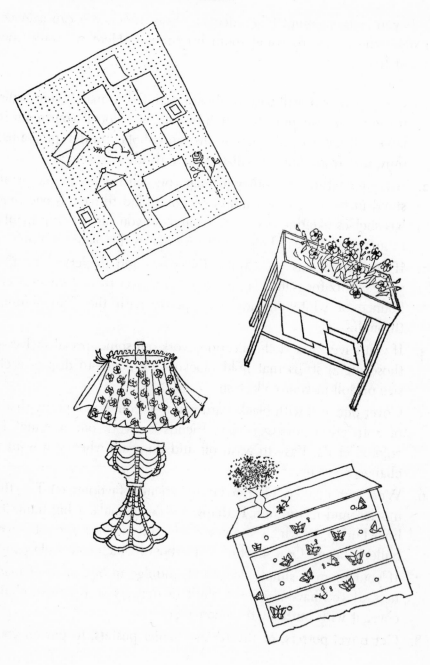

walls with masking tape (masking tape won't pull the paint off when you remove it). You can have very beautiful color pictures this way (especially if you cut off the printing on the posters!).

9. Metal stripping to support bookshelves is available by the foot at hardware stores. It can be cut to fit whatever space you have available in your room, and shelves cut to fit onto it. Try to arrange plants, mementos, and books together on these to give a design effect.

Please don't be discouraged if, six months later, you can't bear the way you've decorated your room. Your taste in the way you'd like the room to look can change far faster than your parents can afford to let you repaint and repaper.

Here, too, like all the other activities of your teens, you are selecting and reselecting as your tastes change and develop. You may range violently in your decorating tastes from French Provincial to Directoire, from Williamsburg to the most advanced of contemporary design. And this is all to your credit. This wandering will help acquaint you with all the riches the field of home beautifying has to offer. In the long run you will learn to appreciate and admire each one so that, if your life falls along lines that require a more traditional approach to decorating, you can live happily. Or if your husband's tastes and your house and community mesh with yours, you may have the most attractive decorating that contemporary design can offer.

John Donne wrote that "no man is an islande." That certainly applies, in a far less spiritual fashion, to the way you decorate both your room as a teen-ager and your home as a wife and mother. A haven for you—and for your family—it surely must be. But a good lesson to learn in your teens is to make the haven all you want it to be, and still let it be part of the mainland of the way your family likes to live—and the way you, as a family, must live in your community.

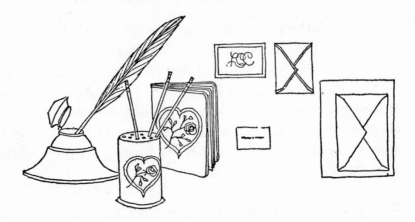

1. *Your Manner*
and Your Manners

YOUR MANNERS are really your manner in action. This whole book is about your manner, but this chapter is about your manners, which reveal your personality, your thoughtfulness, your amiability, your good will to others. About five hundred years ago, Geoffrey Chaucer wrote this line on manners: "That he is gentle that doth gentle deeds." And across the centuries a gentleman—or lady— has been one whose gentle, pleasant manners toward others reflected the kindness and nobility of his nature.

Manners are often called etiquette and, if you look up the word etiquette in a French dictionary, you will find its meaning given as ticket. One of the stories about the word being used to describe polite behavior is that Louis XIV of France was very proud of his lovely gardens and had his troubles keeping the members of the court from trampling his newly seeded lawns. (You probably re-member that in that age the kings kept huge courts in their palaces and members of the court and their families were expected to live in the palace with the king.) Finally, in desperation, the king had his gardener put up warning signs or tickets wherever there was new planting that was to be left undisturbed. He then issued a court order commanding everyone to keep within the *etiquettes*. In a life as formal and precise as that of the French court, keeping within the etiquettes soon became an everyday phrase—meaning to behave properly.

Although the rules of etiquette and, indeed, its meaning have changed since the days of the Sun King, behaving properly, having good manners, is a sure path to success. Good manners smooth your way in life—at home, at school, in your job, your marriage, with your children. More than that, good manners make life pleasanter for the other people in your life. There's a nursery rhyme we learned as little children that puts it very simply and clearly:

> Hearts like doors will ope with ease
> To very, very little keys;
> And don't forget that two of these
> Are "Thank you, sir" and "If you please!"

You will also find that, in addition to opening hearts, the keys of good manners will open many doors all your life. Suppose you and another girl are both being interviewed for a summer job (or to fill the one vacancy still open in the college of your choice, or to get a partial scholarship to an art school). The girl with the better set of manners is more likely to be chosen, assuming that each of you has about the same other qualifications, because people like to have pleasant people around. Keeping within the etiquettes makes the day smoother for everyone. We will talk at greater length about job interviews but you might want to know the few basic rules for the interview we were just thinking about:

1. Find out the name of the person interviewing you.
2. Stand up when she comes in the room.
3. Say, "How do you do, Mrs. Smith; I'm Hope Abbott."
4. Stand until Mrs. Smith sits down—unless she asks you to sit.
5. Put your purse, book on the floor beside your chair so you don't clutter Mrs. Smith's desk—or accidentally walk off with some of her papers.
6. Sit erect with hands folded in lap, ankles crossed.
7. Answer questions clearly, saying, "Yes, Mrs. Smith," "No, Mrs. Smith," when a one-word answer is all that's needed.
8. Wait for Mrs. Smith to conclude the interview.
9. Say, "Thank you very much for seeing me, Mrs. Smith."
10. Say good-by to Mrs. Smith's secretary as you leave.
11. Write a note to Mrs. Smith, thanking her again for seeing you.

Now each of these points is an outward sign of good manners, of consideration for the other person. Mrs. Smith is being kind to interview you, so you learn her name as one way of showing that you appreciate her kindness. You stand up when she comes in the room for the same reason—and because she is your senior in age and position. You sit quietly, because it makes the interview pleasanter and also gives Mrs. Smith a chance to think or to read your résumé without distraction. She has her office arranged to her convenience, so you try not to disturb any of her things. You are appreciative of the time she has spent with you, and you please her by saying so and by your brief note later. And whether or not you get the job, the interview has been a very pleasant fifteen minutes for both you and Mrs. Smith!

The practice of good manners really starts as soon as a baby can lisp out "please" and smile as he reaches for something in his mother's hand. And very soon after he can learn to say "thank you" (or its baby-gabble equivalent!). A few years later, a child is encouraged to shake hands, look at the person he's being introduced to, and say clearly, "How do you do, Mrs. Bennett"; and to say, "Fine, thank you," when asked how he does.

Mothers will remind, over and over again, that the child is to thank both his small friend and his friend's mother for a party or a treat. And, like it or not, he will be urged to send funny drawings or notes to friends or relatives who are ill, thank-you drawings or notes for Christmas and birthday presents. Parents will help a child to learn not to interrupt but to wait for a pause in the conversation and then say, "Excuse me, but may I be excused"—or "have a cake," or "take your pencil," or whatever. A well-taught child learns to eat neatly and inconspicuously; to wear the kind of clothes expected of him; to speak politely to the person who cuts his hair, sells him shoes, and so on. He learns to step aside and let an older person through the door first, to let his guests go first or have first choice, to stand up when adults come in the room or stop by his table at a restaurant.

These are all things your parents try to make second nature to you by the time you reach your teens. And once you've arrived at this brink-of-adulthood stage, there are other things you need to learn once and for all, so that you will do them without thinking twice, without being fearful of doing the "right thing," or being suddenly shy because you're not sure whether you've just made the break of all time. It's a good thing to remember that, if you act out of good will and considerateness, you are more apt than not to do the right thing. But, so you can find your way around the path of the etiquettes, here are some tickets to polite behavior.

73

when you meet people you say, "How do you do," shake hands, and call them by name. You call an adult Mrs. Smith or Mr. Jones, or whatever his name is, unless he asks you to call him by his first name—that is his choice to make, not yours! As you leave a new acquaintance, you say, "It was so nice to see you," or "It's been a great pleasure to meet you," or "I've so enjoyed meeting you."

when you call on the telephone you say, "May I speak to Mrs. Smith, please?" When Mrs. Smith answers, you say, "Good morning, Mrs. Smith. This is Hope Abbott." When you call a friend you say, "May I speak to Jean, please? This is Hope Abbott." You identify yourself because Jean's mother might also be named Jean, so you avoid confusion. And if, on very rare occasions, you are obliged to call a boy, you want to make your call as open and matter-of-fact as possible.

   If Mrs. Smith has called you, you say, "Thank you for calling, Mrs. Smith," rather than, "Good-by, Mrs. Smith."

when you answer the telephone and the call is for you, you answer, "This is Hope Abbott," to the question, "May I speak to Miss Abbott?" (If you recognize a friend calling, of course you say, "This is Hope.") If the call is for someone else who is at home, you say, "May I tell my mother [father, sister, brother] who's calling please?" And if the someone else is not at home, you say, "I'm sorry, my mother isn't home. May I take a message for her, please?" And you write it down!

at home you say, "Good morning," to your family when you arrive at the breakfast table; you say, "Jack, may I have the sugar, please?" When your father comes home from the office, or your mother from a meeting or shopping trip, you stand up and say, "Hello, Mother, I'm glad you're home," or "Hello, Daddy, there's a message for you on the hall table"—or the new sports magazine came today or something to indicate you're interested in him.

at school you say, "Good morning, Miss Wilton," to your teacher; "excuse me," if you bump into someone accidentally; "thank you," if someone helps you with your books or finds something you've dropped. You always look back to see if someone is coming before you let a door swing behind you.

at meals you help seat your mother if your father and brother are not there. You unfold your napkin on your lap; if you are needed to help pass things, you put the napkin, still unfolded, on your chair seat. You use the silver as it's placed on the table—working from the outside in—and you place your knife and fork in the middle of the plate when you're finished (good reason: so they won't slide off when the plate is removed). If you're having soup, an individual casserole, or dessert in a cup-shaped dish that is placed on a plate, you always place your fork or spoon on the plate and never in the cup or casserole (because the spoon is less likely to be struck or spilled if it is flat on the plate). It's a good idea to wipe your mouth with your napkin before drinking from a water glass (because you won't leave an unattractive film on the glass).

If a waitress brings a serving dish to you, you either help yourself or quietly say, "No, thank you." If something is served that you do not or cannot eat, you don't discuss it. You can, to avoid embarrassment, make a pretense of eating some of it.

You try not to spill things, but if you do, don't be the mopper-upper or the picker-upper unless you are at home—and then try to wait till the meal is over. Unless, of course, you've

75

spilled a glass of milk or water. Once you've said you're sorry and the repairs are made, forget the incident.

at a party you first greet all the family before starting any big conversations. You follow the lead of your host or hostess in games, going in for lunch or supper, and so on. When the party is over, you remember your early days and thank both your friend and the parents involved.

out in public you try never to mention the names of people you may be discussing. If you meet friends in a busy store or on a busy shopping street, either speak to them briefly or retire to the nearest soda fountain. You try not to chatter in elevators. You walk on the right-hand side of the sidewalk, leaving the left side for people going the other way. You try to have your fare ready when you board a bus or subway and you move to the rear of the car. Very likely, you would give an older person, or one who is ill, your seat. In stores, you are helpful to the salespeople, stating clearly what you want, making up your mind as soon as possible, and talking as little as possible. You are sure to thank the salesperson, or the hairdresser, or the bus driver who has been helpful to you.

at the movies you say, "excuse me," if you must pass in front of others; and you rise to let others pass in front of you (this is courteous to them and also saves you considerable mashing of dress and feet). You try not to rattle anything—bracelets, beads, popcorn bags, and such—and, although this is a hard one, you do try to talk as little and as quietly as possible.

tipping in restaurants, at the hairdresser, in hotels varies considerably depending on where you live. I have two rules here—one is to give whatever you give with a pleasant smile and say, "thank you"; the other is to ask someone in your family or an older friend what they suggest as a suitable tip for the service rendered.

A general rule in restaurants is 10 to 15 per cent of the bill. On a train, fifty cents to the porter on a day trip, a dollar on an overnight trip. At a hotel or large apartment house, the doorman who gets a cab for you usually receives twenty-five cents, as does the attendant in the powder room at a hotel or restaurant (that is, if she hands you a clean towel, helps brush your dress, or does anything other than just sit there).

compliments are something to be pleased and grateful for, and you need to return the kindness shown you by looking pleased and by saying so. Your answers will vary but they can include "I'm so glad you like it!" "Thank you very much—my aunt just gave it to me and I'm so happy to have it." "How nice of you to tell me!" Say *anything* appreciative, but whatever you do, don't turn the compliment away with some dampening squelch like "Oh, do you like it—my mother says it's awful." "This dress—my sister had it for years." "I can't decide if I like it, I think it makes me look plump." It's true that compliments are often embarrassing—most personal remarks are—but do remember that most compliments are made in the hope of giving you pleasure for something about you or yours that the other person truly admires.

voice is almost more important than what you say. It isn't always the words you utter but your tone of voice that conveys your true meaning. Sometimes words are inadequately chosen for the proper expression, but your intentions will never be misconstrued if your voice portrays a warm, friendly attitude. When

77

being firm in a negative response, don't feel that it is necessary to use short, biting statements; just stick to your point of view and keep your voice pleasant as you make your decision known.

gifts—if you receive a gift of wearing apparel, use it as quickly as is practical in the presence of the donor to show an extra measure of appreciation. Should the gift be of another nature, such as a record or book, refer to it in conversation; or you might relate how the entire family enjoyed the delightful candy you received.

There are a few formal situations that you will also need to know the rules for. These include:

weddings—if you receive an invitation to the reception, you answer it in your best handwriting on your best paper, following the third-person form it was issued in. If you accept, you write (on the first page *only*):

Miss Hope Abbott
accepts with pleasure
Mr. and Mrs. Henry Hartwell's
kind invitation for
Tuesday, the fourth of October

If you cannot go, you write:

Miss Hope Abbott
regrets she is unable to accept
Mr. and Mrs. Henry Hartwell's
kind invitation for
Tuesday, the fourth of October

Until you have answered a good many formal invitations, I think it's a good money-saving idea to write out your answer once on a piece of scratch paper cut the same size as your writing paper. That way you will be sure you can space the lines properly and get all the words in.

If you are invited to the reception or breakfast after the wedding, you will need to send a present to the bride. If you are invited only to the wedding, you don't need to send a present.

If you have never gone to a wedding before, it will help you to know that your usual procedure for a large formal wedding is like this:

1. An usher meets you at the entrance and offers his arm. If you are to be seated in the pews in front that are reserved for the family and closest friends, you either present a card or tell the usher your pew number. . . . If not, he will ask you whether you prefer to sit on the bride's side of the church or the groom's.
2. After the ceremony, the ushers escort the ladies in the family pews, beginning with the bride's mother, to the door, while all other guests stay in their places until this ceremony has been accomplished.

Weddings, large or small, are conducted on some variation of this principle—someone will meet you, guide you, place you; and your best cue is to move slowly and to observe what the other guests are doing.

paper work—letter writing will be a part of your path of etiquettes all your life. A very useful feminine accomplishment is pretty handwriting, and this is an art you will need to perfect if it is to be yours. Whether the style that pleases you is upright, backhand, cursive, or manuscript writing is unimportant; you do need to use good spacing, good margins, and make your writing legible through the actual writing and through your choice of pen and paper—or typewriter, since all but the most formal of invitations, acceptances, or regrets can be typed.

The kind of writing paper you buy will—obviously!—depend on your taste. But please do remember that your letters are *you*, they represent you, they speak for you when you are not there. The classic choice in writing paper is a smooth-surfaced white kid, either single or double-folded sheets that fold in half to go into a square envelope. Gray, pastel-blue, or pin-striped blue or gray paper are all in good taste. You will see many other colors on display, so a good shopping hint is to remember that the more the paper departs from the classic styles, the less useful it will be to you—and the more unusual the color or design, the more you will have to pay to get both good quality paper and striking design.

Half-size paper is often used for short notes or invitations, and post cards printed with your address are convenient. If you type a great many letters, you can find handsome large-sheet paper in conservative colors and textures.

Black ink is the most correct, but many people prefer blue, green, or violet.

We will talk more about special letters you write in the chapters on getting along with girls and with boys, but these basic rules apply to all letters:

1. Make your letters as neat and attractive-looking as you can.

2. If your address is not printed or engraved on the paper, be sure to write it in at the end of the letter on the left-hand side of the paper, just below the date.

3. Letters to friends should begin with "Dear Mary" and close with "Sincerely," "Fondly," "Affectionately," "Devotedly," "Love," or "Best."

4. Letters to non-friends (possible employers, schools, stores) should begin "Dear Sir" (or "Dear Sirs") and close "Yours truly" or "Very truly yours."

5. You sign your name, "Hope Abbott," if the letter is to someone you don't know very well or if it is to non-friends (see 4); in other cases, you sign simply, "Hope." If you wish, you may add (Miss) in parentheses to the left of your signature in a non-friend business letter. I can think of only one situation where that would be really necessary, and that would be if your first name could be used for either a boy or girl (like Brooks, Leslie, Sydney, Gene).

6. You use no abbreviations on the envelopes if at all possible. If your writing paper doesn't have your address on the envelope, you write your name and address on the back flap of the envelope.

Here's the way you would address an envelope to each member of a family of your friends, the Browns:

person	how he or she would sign a letter to you	how you would address a letter to him or her
mother	Jean Tibbett Brown	Mrs. Howard Kerr Brown
father	Howard K. Brown	Mr. Howard K. Brown
sister	Jean	Miss Jean Grimes Brown
older brother	Howard	Mr. Howard K. Brown, Jr.
small brother	Tibby	Master Tibbett Grimes Brown

Here is a small portfolio of sample letters for you to adapt to your own manner and your own reason for writing the type of letter involved.

THE SITUATION:

> Mrs. Brown, Jean's mother, has invited you to a lunch she is giving.

THE INVITATION:

> Dear Hope:
> Will you come to lunch on Saturday, the sixth of January, at one o'clock?
> The junior committee for the Valentine's Dance will have its first meeting after lunch, and I'm looking forward to seeing you all then.
>
> Very sincerely,
Jean Tibbett Brown
>
> December twenty-eighth

THE ACCEPTANCE:

Dear Mrs. Brown:

Thank you very much for asking me to lunch on Saturday the sixth at one o'clock.

I'm delighted to be on the Junior Committee and all this makes it seem very grown up and wonderful to me!

Affectionately,
Hope

December 30th

THE REGRET:

Dear Mrs. Brown:

I am sorry I can't come for lunch and the committee meeting on the sixth.

That is the week-end Daddy is taking us all to Uncle Dick's for three days of skiing.

If there is anything I can do beforehand to help with the meeting, please let me know.

With best thanks,
Affectionately,
Hope

December 30th

84

THE SITUATION:

> Mrs. Robinson, Jean's aunt whom you have never met, has invited you to a tea for Jean's sister, whose engagement has just been announced.

THE INVITATION:

> Dear Hope:
>
> Will you come to a tea for my niece, Melissa Brown, on Friday, January nineteenth, from four until six o'clock?
>
> I am looking forward to the pleasure of meeting you.
>
> > Very sincerely,
> > Melissa Grimes Robinson

January fourth
130 Wildwood Terrace

THE ACCEPTANCE:

Dear Mrs. Robinson:

Thank you
for asking me to your tea for
Melissa on Friday the nineteenth
at four o'clock.

It will be a
great pleasure to come — and
I'm so looking forward to
meeting you.

Sincerely,

Hope Abbott

January 6th

THE REGRET:

Dear Mrs. Robinson:

I am so sorry I won't be able to come to your tea for Melissa on Friday the nineteenth.

That is the afternoon of my mid-year exam in chemistry and it starts at four o'clock.

Thank you for your kindness in asking me to come — it would have been a great treat.

Sincerely,

Hope Abbott

January 6th

87

THE SITUATION:

Mrs. Smith of the Weber Company interviewed you
yesterday for a summer job. You want to thank her.

Mrs. Burton Smith
Personnel Director
The Weber Company
145 Market Street
Fairfield, Ohio
Dear Mrs. Smith:

    I so appreciate your
seeing me yesterday, and I feel
I learned a great deal about the
Weber Company. If I'm lucky
enough to work there this summer
I know I will have done a great
deal to make my college life and
future career more worthwhile.

    With many thanks for your
kindness,

        Very truly yours,

        Hope Abbott

April 27, 1957
18 Rockrow Place
Fairfield, Ohio

THE SITUATION:

You want to order by mail from a store in New York.

Murray Brothers
1400 Broad St
New York, New York
Dear Sirs:

      I would like to order one of the dacron shirtmaker dresses you advertised on Sunday January 14, 1957 in the New York Times. It was from the Junior Department, Fifth Floor.

      Please send me model A in size nine in navy blue priced at $14.95, and charge it to my mother's account.

         Yours truly,
         Hope Abbott

Charge address:
Mrs. Sheldon A. Abbott
18 Rockrose Place
Fairfield, Ohio

THE SITUATION:

    A friend is ill and in the hospital.

Dear Jeanie:

    I'm as sorry as I can be about your losing your appendix. I wish I could have held your hand — not that anyone would have let me, I expect.

    Your mother tells me you are not to have visitors for a few days but she said I could come over as soon as Dr. Vincent says it's all right. Meantime I thought you would enjoy the new Langley novel so I will send it along.

    Please let me know if there is anything I can do to help- school, dance, any chore at all.

        Affectionately

        Hope

March 12th

90

THE SITUATION:

A friend has lost a young aunt who was very close to her.

Dear Anne:

Melissa just called to tell me about your aunt, and I'm as sorry as I can be. I think I loved Claire almost as much as you did – she was always so wonderful to me.

I will write to Charlie right away. I feel so bad about him because they both had such a splendid life together and so many plans.

With much love,

Hope

June 6th

THE SITUATION:

Your favorite teacher, Mrs. Ellis, has just had her first child.

Dear Mrs. Ellis:

We talked of nothing else in class yesterday but your new little daughter! Melissa said she weighed almost seven pounds and that you and Mr. Ellis have named her Elizabeth. What a lovely name!

When she is old enough to be admired Joan and I would love to come and see her.

We have all missed you very much this year and hope Elizabeth realizes how lucky she is to have you around all day.

Please remember our training as baby sitters — we'd be honored to stay with Elizabeth.

Devotedly, Hope

Getting along with the people who make up your world can be a long and lasting pleasure if you realize the ease and happiness others derive from your amiable manner and considerate manners. And that happiness will be returned to you a hundredfold.

*Getting Along
With Girls*

1. *Breaking Through the Shyness Barrier*

EVERYONE is shy. Not all the time, not always in the same situation. But the most self-assured, brilliant, gregarious person you know probably has a bout or two of shyness every week of his or her life—and no one else may ever know it! No one can help feeling shy, but everyone *can* do something to meet and overcome the attack. It's a little like swallowing down the "wrong throat" or choking—you don't *plan* to do it. Doctors tell you to raise your left hand straight to the ceiling to relax your diaphragm and stop the spasm of choking. And when you suddenly have a spasm of shyness, you need to have a remedy to ease you over the bad moment.

But first, what is shyness? There are many ways to describe it—a shrinking that comes from inexperience, an overwhelming nervousness, skittishness, timidness—but it seems to me that calling it a barrier that is suddenly raised by your nervous system between you and the person you want to talk to comes closer to describing the feeling of shyness. You can be shy with someone you have just met, with someone you have known a long time but whom you meet in a new situation, with someone you admire, with someone you love. It isn't that you don't want to talk to the person you are shy with; the very intensity of your desire to communicate helps increase your shyness. And when you consider that other people are often shy, too, you can imagine how high a barrier may suddenly rise between two people!

You can also become extremely shy in a new situation—your first days at a new school, when you first move to a new neighborhood, when you first go by yourself to a tea party, on your first date with a new beau, at your first job interview.

Everyone wants to look and act well in the eyes of others; and when you face a battery of new situations, you may become self-conscious about the way you look, walk, eat, maneuver a teacup—about what you say and whether you are talking too rapidly or in too loud a voice. You shouldn't, of course. Part of the great charm of youth is its April quality of exuberance and quiet, of heart-catching grace and equally entrancing awkwardness, of complete assurance and fawnlike uncertainty.

You've seen your small brothers or sisters hiding behind your mother's skirts—or peeping through their fingers when they are shy—and you realize that, although they are shy, it doesn't bother them. But you, nearing adulthood, realize that visible shyness is not a social grace and that because of it you may lose a chance to make a new friend, attract a new beau, go to a party.

You don't try to stop being shy (any more than you try to change the color of your eyes or the fact that you weep at sad movies), but you do try to develop some positive action to take so that the shyness will not be awkward for others and will not build a barrier between you and new people and new situations.

Keeping some of these points in mind should help:

- Slow down and breathe easily when you enter a crowded room, when you are in any new situation.

- Be sure you stand erectly with your head up—you'll look assured, even if you're not!

- If you have bought new clothes for the occasion, wear the entire outfit at least once beforehand. That way you'll be aware of all the things that might plague you—the too-long slip, the bra strap that shows, the hook that hangs by a thread, the pretty little hat that won't stay anchored to your head without two hatpins (it came with only *one*).

- For any new situation, dress simply and carry as few things as possible. Try not to have packages or books to worry about. And this is the time to have a purse with a handle that goes over your arm and leaves you with two hands free.

- Move slowly enough so your coat won't catch on tables or doors or sweep things off low tables. Get up from a chair easily, making sure your heel doesn't catch in the hem of your dress or coat.

- When you are sitting, look serene by being still—no twisting a lock of hair, turning a bracelet or ring, twirling a scarf, tugging at a skirt.

- When you are eating, take small bites, chew slowly; first rest your hand on the implement or glass instead of grabbing it up. Take a sip of water before speaking.

- When you're not sure what is expected of you in a new situation, look around the room and take your cue from the others—and don't hesitate to ask someone near you. Asking someone to help you is a good way to start a conversation and perhaps to make a new friend. (You remember the old joke about everybody loving to give advice and nobody wanting to take it.)

Often you can bypass an attack of shyness by being kind to others. A good guest helps her hostess by circulating around the room, trying to talk a little while with each person there. And if you have come with a boy, you help him—and your hostess—to enjoy the party more if you talk to the other guests.

Perhaps your hostess introduced you to one or two people when you came in, but now the groups have shifted and you and Steve—the boy who brought you—are talking to each other. This is not desperate, and there's no reason why you shouldn't talk together. But after five minutes or so of this, you can say, "There's a nice-looking girl who just came in. Let's go and talk to her." Then you hold out your hand, say, "How do you do, I'm Jane Jones. Do you know Steve Jenkins?" Or if you know the girl, you say, "Hello, Lucy, it's nice to see you. Do you know Steve Jenkins?" After she and Steve have said how-do-you-do, you can bring up a subject you and Steve were talking about—the basketball team, the new baseball coach, the new movie, the strawberry festival at the church (whatever interested you and Steve is likely to interest another young person). And while you don't give a stranger the third degree, there's no reason why you shouldn't show an interest in her by asking if she goes to your school or if she's known your hostess a long time.

If she is thoroughly uncommunicative, you and Steve can move along to another group and start the whole process all over again. You can't run into a sphinx very often!

However, if she says, "Oh, I met Mary two years ago when she came to the Hopkins School," then you ask her if she is returning the visit for a special event your school may be having. If it's just a social visit, tell her you hope she'll come often. You might touch on the sports programs at your school versus the programs at her school—this will also keep Steve engaged and interested in the conversation.

It's always a good idea to let others talk as much as possible. People like being listened to and are always glad of a new audience! But they like an interested listener, one who asks leading questions. Good leading-question material can always be found in the newspaper. You might comment on a front-page event of local or national scope— you can always engender excitement by being well versed in the happenings of the day, and the people you are talking to are bound to have two or three personal comments on a generally known subject.

Good conversational material can also be found in your classroom, your neighborhood. You might have something to contribute along these lines: "The geometry test caused havoc in class today. We haven't learned yet whether we'll all have to review the work. Have you ever had your whole class fail an exam?" Or, "Jerry Shea was telling me that spraying trees and crops actually affects human beings, and the poison in the air or on foods could make us ill. We've just had the shade trees sprayed in our neighborhood, and Jerry thinks we should have committees to alert people to these dangers." You will find people are enchanted at an opportunity to view with alarm or to join in a discussion of how something could be done better.

Books, plays, and movies are always welcome subjects. For even if the others haven't read the books or seen the shows, the casts and stories make excellent conversational fare. Please don't tell the outcome unless you're prodded to do so—it will spoil the pleasure of anticipation for the others. However, you can define what you liked or disliked about segments or about the work as a whole. And you can always discuss the art direction or the appearance of the book.

Actually, the simplest way to practice the art of conversation is with your parents' friends, and perhaps your mother will let you help with her next afternoon party. You already know much of the circumstances of family friends without realizing it, and she will probably tell you a little about any new people who are coming. You will want to listen politely when you join any group, find out what is being discussed, and, if you have a pertinent question to ask or piece of information to give, you can join in. If you don't, you can be interested.

101

murmur, "Isn't that interesting," or "How fascinating," and be a good audience thereby. And while you are being a good audience, you can observe how others contribute to the conversation—keeping it going, saying something light to break up a tense moment, smoothly turning the conversation to another subject if the one under discussion is obviously painful or unpleasant to someone in the group.

One good thing to know is that if you should make some great blunder during a conversation (and there's no reason why you shouldn't, since all of us do every so often), there's no point in being miserable or worrying over it. Notice how often you hear others saying, "I said the most stupid thing..." or "I made the worst break..." or "I really didn't mean to say that...."

It's a good idea to practice any mannerisms, ways of talking, voice improvement, or special "tricks" you may have picked up from others, in the privacy of your room or with your mother or trusted sister as an audience. Better not let the girls you know in on these sessions, for your best friend today may not be tomorrow and she might embarrass you by letting others in on your secret. And don't be self-conscious about deliberately practicing self-improvement. Doctors concerned with mental health, whose degrees would fill a chest, have long agreed that "acting out" your anxieties and "acting in" your new situations are mighty healthy things to do.

Remember, shyness is your inability to communicate the inner you whom you are anxious to have people know. You might look at the problem of shyness from a different point of view: the ideal in life is to have self-approval—if you don't like yourself why should anyone else bother to? In the sureness of self-approval, you are able to express your self by words and gestures that are completely in accord as you meet life's situations. Like all ideals, this is a goal to work toward—it is the perfection we all seek. When you observe the adults around you, you will recognize that only some have attained that goal. But you are moving toward it; and since your learning process is far more rapid during your teen years, far more keen in its perception of self, you will do more to set your adult patterns of communication now than in later years. Frequently, during these years, you can waste energy berating yourself for the things you should have done, the things you should have said. When you can reach the stage of knowing that you did the best you could at the moment—and then go on to forget the error and concentrate on the lesson learned—you will be taking one of your largest steps toward maturity.

A grand tool to chip away at your shyness is your own sense of humor. Give it a chance by laughing at yourself and the fixes you get into, and you will find all tensions eased around you. If your spoon slips and the meringue glacée lands in your lap, a quick mop-up job is, of course, in order. But more important is the fact that your humorous comments and laughing acceptance of your problem will quickly ease the awkward situation, bring a sunburst of sympathetic smiles, and make you many new friends. The whole party could have been spoiled if you had brooded over your mishap. Turning it into a fun situation which other people can laugh about is the ideal, but if you can't manage that, do the next best thing: simply keep quiet. And if you break your hostess's favorite record or vase, apologize to the owner and let it go at that. If your friends make you the butt of a joke, at least try to smile even if you can't manage a rebuttal. With some people, joking at another's expense is almost an affectionate gesture—they think you like the attention. They are hurt if you suddenly grow huffy over a particularly sensitive soft spot peculiar to you.

One charming amusing man I know has a philosophy about jokes that is worthy of note. It's this: Never be as funny as you can at the expense of others. If you can tell a joke that's on you, fine. If it's at someone else's expense, stop. To those who are bright and quick, the humor of other people's foibles and shortcomings is almost irresistibly funny, but kindness and courtesy both require you to curb the temptation to tease.

Everyone wants to be part of a crowd. This is acceptance; and when you have acceptance, there is a wonderful feeling of belonging. But when you are shy, you—and every member of your crowd, as you will gradually discover—have special problems to which you will be particularly sensitive at different ages.

When you are a very young teen-ager, handling friendships with girls is a very real, sometimes heartbreaking, experience. You may be hurt because you have been very close to a girl who suddenly finds another girl more fun. You, in turn, may find that suddenly your interests seem exactly the opposite from those of the girl who has been nearest and dearest to you. She ceases to be interesting to you, and you begin to break away by forming a friendship with another girl or possibly two or three other girls. You are all merely growing up and learning that you want around you those who have something in common—mutual projects, people, opinions.

As you get older, you discover that you are growing less and less capable of sustaining interest in only one person, and you long to be part of a group. Getting into the crowd may present a problem to you if you are particularly shy. The quickest and surest way is through the girls you know individually who mix well with others. Giving parties to which these girls are invited, going with them to the drugstore or other meeting places, will gradually get you accepted by new groups. One sure way of getting yourself disliked is by being openly critical, particularly of girls obviously well liked. Just as you'll be shifting back and forth from one crowd to another, so do others. Nothing kills your chances for easy friendships more than the knowledge that you gossip, criticize, or are maliciously "superior."

Your talents and your interests are the magic key which can unlock the door to any group activity. If you dance well, you'll be in demand to teach your friends the steps that they find difficult but you learn easily. If you play the piano or other instruments, if you have a record collection, if you are particularly adept at decorating or sketching, your interests will stimulate others to emulate or admire your talents. These talents add immeasurably to your own identity as an individual. If reading is your hobby, you are lucky, too, for you'll find it not only enriches your life by taking you into other worlds and enlarging your scope, but it widens your lines of communication to others and is an invaluable aid to your personal success.

Here are ways to overcome shyness. Try one today, and tomorrow you may want to try another. Remember, we all take two steps forward and one step backward every now and then, so don't get discouraged if your first attempts at friendliness fail:

- Instead of smiling at an acquaintance, stop and speak.
- Smile at a girl or boy whom you've seen frequently but whose presence you have not acknowledged before.
- Volunteer to help on a committee where help is needed.
- Learn a new dance step and teach it to one of your friends.
- If you are adept at sketching, drawing, or painting, volunteer to make decorations or place cards or something which will contribute to a gathering.
- If you read for pleasure, discuss a book you've enjoyed with a friend. Or if you've seen a television show or a play that interested you, find someone who's also seen the show and discuss it.
- Participate in some sports activity. If you don't play volley ball, softball, basketball, tennis, or badminton, learn how. People, in general, are flattered by the opportunity to teach a game or a skill in which they excel.
- Try introducing an old friend to a person she hasn't met.
- Smile each time you begin to speak. You will look more pleasant and you will have a positive approach to what you are going to say.

Shyness is an awkward feeling you will experience in some degree and on some occasions all your life. But if you will meet it with courage and good humor—recognizing that it is a very ordinary feeling that seems extraordinary only when it happens to you—you can easily break through the shyness barrier. Once you've learned this, friends are yours for the asking.

2. Friends for the Asking

LOOKING into a microscope is an engrossing occupation that reveals whole new worlds of beauty and knowledge; and each time I see an apparently dull, lifeless slide come alive under a microscope, I marvel at how everything living is in motion—a drop of water crowded with tiny molecules that group and regroup, a minute insect that turns out to have hundreds of legs all bicycling rapidly, a mold that teems with life-saving organisms such as those that go to make up penicillin.

Your first impression of a newborn baby is that it sleeps without budging for hours between feedings. If you can, watch the baby for ten or fifteen minutes and you'll discover that it is never still even while asleep.

The world, so full of life, is moving; and adult, adolescent, or child—your personal world is always in motion, too. Adults often complain that the world is moving too fast! But to impatient adolescents, whose dreams are so immense, the world may seem to be standing still—and you sometimes feel that instead of being on a world that spins, you are pin-pointed on a flat blue-vaulted space in an endless sameness of time.

Then when your world does start spinning, it comes as something of a shock to you. Perhaps your father's job changes and you move to another town—or your family moves from the city to the suburbs—or you finish grade school and all your friends disperse to many different high schools, to private schools, or to boarding schools. Your spinning world is exciting, there are new places to go, new things to do, new challenges to enjoy, and—most exciting of all—new friends who are yours for the asking.

Old friends?—you'll keep up with them, of course, as time and distance permit. There are some people you can see after several years have passed and still feel comfortable with them and close in spirit. Others drift away and, while you both regret it, that friendship is replaced by others.

But people, most people—perhaps all people!—are wonderful and, whether you stay in your town or whether you move to new places every few years, you will find that one of the major pleasures of life is that there are always new friends to make, new people with new ideas who will open new worlds to you.

Friendship breeds friendship, it is an art; and once you have learned how to be a friend, you can't fail to have friends in whatever path your life may take you. In the medical world, people who frequently burn or cut themselves or frequently fall or stumble and get hurt—for many reasons, including a hunger for sympathy and attention from others—are described as "*accident-prone*." There's a certain charm in that phrase that we can put to happier use. *You can, if you*

108

wish, be friendship-prone. And, to be friendship-prone, you have to wish two things—one, to make friends; and, two, to keep them.

We'll talk about keeping friends in the next chapter. In this one, let's consider ways to make friends.

The girls and boys next door   On the whole, just as the boy next door is likely to make the best husband for you, the girls and boys next door are probably your first and best choice in friends. They are near, so you will have more chances to talk, play, study with them. You will probably go to the same schools, use the same tennis courts, and so on. Your parents either have met or will meet their parents. Usually, people in the same neighborhood have an equality of interests, standards, and goals that makes for pleasant, comfortable friendship. And so the grownups will probably include the young people in some of their activities and plan other activities especially for their teen-agers.

How to meet the young people in your neighborhood? Do you remember in *Little Women* how the March girls met Laurie, the boy next door who opened so many new worlds for them? Laurie was ill with a bad throat, and Jo, who had never met him, saw him looking out his bedroom window and looking rather forlorn at that; so she smiled and waved as she was romping around the garden between her family's little house and his grandfather's big house. A simple, from-a-kind-heart gesture—she was out having fun, he was inside and ill—that brought much eventual happiness to many lives.

So when you are trundling the cart to the supermarket, or out playing or digging in the garden, or walking with your small brother or sister—or your dog—you can smile and say hello to the boys and girls who, you know, live in your neighborhood. And if you look bright and happy, they'll probably speak to you first because it's fun to have a nice newcomer to make friends with.

Then you go to your church where your parents will introduce the family to the minister, priest, or rabbi. When your mother has time, she'll probably join some of the women's activities and you will meet other young people through her. But until she can, see what young people's activities—both religious and social—you can enter into in your place of worship.

If it's summertime, there's a wealth of recreational opportunities that will help you find friends. Start with your family. Your father, mother, brother, or sister might take you to play golf or tennis or to some of the local baseball games; you're sure to meet people there, or on the way. Perhaps there's a lake, river, or beach where you could swim. Or a swimming pool or a club your parents might be willing and able to join. Perhaps there's a picnic spot or a park where your family could go for a cook-out. And you as a family can have a great deal of fun right at home that your neighbors can see and want to join—a cook-out, a badminton or croquet set, a basketball area, a tennis backboard to practice against, a shuffleboard court, a big collapsible swimming pool, or just a hose spray.

The point of all this is that if you are obviously having a good time at whatever you are doing, others will think you must be fun to have around and they will want to meet you. Conversely, if by any chance you feel and look discouraged about being new and not knowing anyone, you are not very likely to have anyone beating a path to your door to get to know you. You have to be *somebody* and do *something!*

Other things you might well do would include community activities. Perhaps there is a settlement house or well-baby clinic or community playground where you could volunteer your services—even if the best you feel you can do is to pour fruit juice or put away playground equipment (somebody has to pour fruit juice or put away playground equipment). Any of the dozens of civic, social, and community activities in your town will find a job for an interested volunteer, and that's a much better way to spend your time than staying home looking wistful.

Or you might learn something special. It isn't very often in life that one is given a present of time to spend lavishly in developing a special skill. Perhaps you have longed to play the guitar or a really good game of tennis or to dive or to typewrite. This is your chance. And if your family can't afford to underwrite the whole cost of these lessons, you might get a part-time job at the supermarket or drugstore or in a dress shop—or do an organized job of getting so many hours of baby-sitting a week—to help pay for your lessons. By fall you will have accomplished three things: you'll have developed a special skill that will make you more of a personality in your new school; you'll have the satisfaction of having done something constructive with your time; and you will have met many new people both through your lessons and through your part-time summer job.

So much for the summer!

Here you are, about to make the big plunge into a new school— new teachers, new subjects, new projects, new friends. You are about to make a big investment of your time, your energy, your talents, and your heart. No wise person invests carelessly. You've heard your parents talk about a new car being a big investment and you've seen them shop around for the model they thought would bring them the greatest return for their investment. You've been with your mother when she's been shopping for a new sofa or a new coat and you've observed the care and thought she's expended before making her choice.

You, in a new school situation, are in a sense shopping, too. If you buy hastily, you may regret your choice—but it's not easy to credit a set of friends or school activities, particularly since the follies of a hasty choice may not be apparent to you for a few months.

I would think that in order to make the best friends possible at a new school you would start out with two immediate goals. The first, to look and act as pretty, neat, and pleasant as possible, and to do as well as possible in your studies (without being ostentatious about it). The second, to become acquainted with as many people as possible. There's a significant difference in becoming acquainted with people and in becoming friends with them. Looking up the original meanings or derivations of words can teach us a good deal. Acquaint, for example, weaves its meaning back through Old French to Middle English to the Latin verb that is translated *to know*. Friend, on the other hand, comes from the Anglo-Saxon word *frēogan*, which means *to love*. And, despite the old song, to know someone is not necessarily to love that someone.

So shop for a while before you invest in friends. Have a cheery smile and friendly word for the boys and girls in your class—the long, the short, the tall, the fat, the thin, the friendly, the reserved. Do something helpful for them when you can. Circulate as much as possible until you are sure of the ones you want for your friends. For a time, try to sit next to different people in your various classes, try to eat with different groups, try to walk home with an assortment of boys and girls. Go to school meetings, be interested but postpone joining any clubs or organizations. (Like all hard and fast statements, there are exceptions, of course, to that last one. If you want —more than almost anything else—to work on the school paper, grab the opportunity if it comes your way or if you can maneuver it. If you want to play in the school band or on the tennis team, don't dally if you're offered the chance. But, *in general*, go slowly in signing yourself up for activities you may want to drop later.)

To have a friend, you must be a friend—so now that you have made a number of acquaintances in your new home or new school, let's consider the ways friendships can be made to last.

112

3. *Friends for Keeps*

EACH ERA of life has its jewels of love, accomplishment, beauty, and dignity; and one of the more charming jewels of maturity is the glow that comes from friendships. You've probably heard the adults in your family say things along these lines: "Janet Stone? Why, we've been friends since we were little girls!" "Mary Brocton and I have been dear friends since we were in school together!" "The Laines? They've been our close friends all our married lives!"

A lasting friendship has its elements of love, beauty, and dignity—and especially of accomplishment, because a friendship that lasts never "just happens." The friends you make now may not all be lasting ones, but with each friendship you are developing your talent in this important part of the structure of your personality and of a happy life. To have a friend, you must be a friend. That means effort on your part. You learn to share your ideas and talents, to help your friends when they need help—whether it's a hurried assist in turning up the hem of a bouffant dance dress, trying to understand the math assignment, or untangling the conjugation of French verbs; patching up a quarrel with a beau, lending books and records, or taking care of a young brother so a friend can try out for the school play.

You sometimes have to forego the things you want to do because you can't always have things just the way you would like them. Not in friendship, school, business, marriage, or motherhood! There is much give-and-take in any good relationship and this teaches you to arbitrate both your wishes and your differences.

A good friendship is a creative undertaking. You learn from each other—sports, hobbies, study, entertaining, part-time jobs. You take on new projects like cooking, dressmaking, painting, or making jewelry because each friend gives the other the incentive to do a little more and a little better. You draw other friends into your activities because the enthusiasm you generate is catching.

And you do things for others. If your aunt or your friend's older sister has a new baby, you offer to do the shopping or you and your friend make up several casserole meals so the new mother has more time to relax and enjoy her baby. Or you help another friend paint her room. Or you make Christmas baskets for the church to distribute, or you do some community work. If you know the way they like it done, you delight and astonish your fathers by washing their cars some Saturday. Or you volunteer to set out the tulip bulbs for both your houses.

There are other elements of friendship that require creative activity on your part, too. Loyalty is a must in all human relationships. You won't always agree with another person and you won't always like the other person. Sometimes a great difference of opinion and the settling of the difference give a friendship new strength and value. Back in the seventeenth century the famous English clergyman and scholar, Robert Burton, wrote a line so true that it has been used over and over again; he said, "The falling out of lovers is the renewing of love." But when you have a falling out, you have an obligation to yourself and to your friend, and that obligation involves not criticizing her, not revealing secrets she has entrusted to you; and it involves not saying anything if you can't say something good!

Reliability is another important quality to friendship, and it's sometimes a difficult one to maintain. It means keeping your promises if you can—or explaining why you can't keep them; it means doing the things you agree to do—or explaining why you can't do them. It means returning things you borrow and returning them in good condition. It means meeting people on time or letting them know if you'll be late. But it also has some deeper meanings and these include a reliability of disposition—being good-tempered and agreeable, being honest and open, having the courage to bring up and discuss things that are bothering you, and having the good humor and good sense to mend your ways if some of the things you do make your friends unhappy.

Reliability also includes knowing what your own standards of behavior and ethics are, and sticking to them. There are many sets of rules to follow, from the Ten Commandments to the Girl Scout code. Know your own code well and live by it. And put a postscript to the code that tells you to be critical of the way you live up to your own standards and to be compassionate of the way others live up to their standards—or to *your* standards. You don't need to approve of what others do, you don't need to go along with them or to associate with them, but you do need to let them have the privileges of making their own mistakes.

No one is always lucky, either in love or in friendship. Not all friendships are for keeps, and this is a good thing to learn early in life. You will surely outgrow many of the friendships you make, now and in the future. You need to learn to be easygoing about it; other friendships will come along. And when one you value dissolves abruptly or slowly drifts away, remember that this is a sadness that everyone experiences and that it's part of being a member of the adult world. Friendships break up for many reasons. You move away, you go to a different school, the family fortunes change and you have to drop out of a number of activities that are both fun and costly; these are the easy reasons to understand. A little less easy is the outgrowing of a friendship. Here it's important to remember that, calendar age to the contrary, not everyone develops at the same pace. Just like your mother's garden, there are those who bloom early and those who bloom late—just as there are crocuses and chrysanthemums, blondes, brunettes, and redheads. A girl who has been your good friend may disappear out of your life—perhaps the interests you shared suddenly seem juvenile to her. She may have grown away from you and need more adult interests; she may have a job that takes up her spare time; she may be fascinated with a new hobby that bores you; she may find that she would rather spend her spare time with beaux than with you and other girls; the reasons are manifold.

Now is the time to recognize that some friendships fade into an acquaintanceship that can be a pleasant one if you make it so. The world is so blessed with pleasant people and pleasant activities that it is foolish to waste a moment's energy on hurt feelings or unpleasantness. If you do, you will be the loser.

Sometimes you will find yourself involved in friendships you don't want to keep. Girls—and boys, too,—who lack the same standards you and your family think are desirable, those whom you would be ashamed to bring to a family gathering, those who would earn (and probably deserve) your family's disapproval because of their bad manners, snobbishness, slovenliness, ultrasophistication—whatever the reason is—are better discarded than held on to with blind devotion. True, they may demand your loyalty, but it is quixotic of you to give it. The rebels in the world are fun, they are often exciting, but the Damon and Pythias legend can really be quite a bore when you think of the fun, pleasure, and general approval it can cost you.

There will always be people who criticize others who conform to accepted standards of behavior; but, actually, the one mistake you can make here is to conform to the point of losing your identity. Within limits, most people conform to accepted codes of behavior; and within the prescribed framework of accepted customs they develop individual tastes. The more we project ourselves as individuals, the more we will set ourselves apart from the average. In this very rugged and competitive world, it is the individuals who set new patterns of procedure—within existing codes—who become the leaders. These, then, are the successful people. But it is a rare occasion indeed when a complete nonconformist is able to set himself apart as an object of admiration. More likely, he is considered something of a freak.

When you find yourself unhappily involved with a group or a person you would like to break free of, how do you go about it? You can't set yourself up as a moral arbiter no matter how much you disapprove of the group's activities—whether they include reckless driving, parties that last too long and too late and too unchaperoned, going to parties at places your families disapprove, or whatever the major or minor crime is. Your problem is to break away, not to reform. Here are some steps to take which you can modify to suit the situation:

1. Refuse any and all invitations with a firm, friendly "Thank you, but I'm sorry I can't come." Excuses, discussions of why you can't come will get you nowhere. A polite no and a pleasant smile are all you have to offer.

117

2. Don't gossip about the activities of the group—remember, there are few situations in life that are actually black or white.

3. Be wary of criticizing any individual member of the group. You can't tell if she might be as bored with the group's activities as you are; she might become your brother's best girl in six months' time and you'd have a fine family situation on your hands if you'd alienated her with idle chatter.

4. If you sincerely disapprove of the girl or the group with good reason, you'd be wise to become very involved with a bevy of activities so you won't be lured back into the group out of sheer loneliness.

5. Be chary of joining another group. You might be better off with a few stanch friends from the boy-and-girl-next-door group who may not be glamorous but whose steadiness makes up for your young and sometimes wobbly judgment about people.

Friendships *are* jewels in your life. All the cutting and polishing in the world won't make a chunk of glass into a diamond. Some friendships are semiprecious, and although you would never make a major investment in a moonstone or a topaz, these lovely, delicate, shimmering stones have their own lighthearted beauty and can give you much pleasure. You will learn to recognize the more permanent jewels and to give them the care and affection they deserve and the respect they merit for their more durable fire.

4. *Pride and Prejudice*

IF EVER a country and its people had the privilege and the obligation to be without prejudice, ours is that country. There probably has never been a land so richly endowed with people of so many races, religions, and national backgrounds with so magnificent an opportunity to know and appreciate one another's cultures and beliefs.

Radio, television, movies, the laws of the land, and the universal military training our young men—and often their young families—experience, all are serving to drive the ugly emotion of prejudice from our hearts and minds. Prejudice is a lack of knowledge, an unreasonable objection, a preconceived judgment without just grounds. The better born and bred a person is, the less prejudiced he is.

What does prejudice mean? It's a good deal more, actually, than being "against" those of a different race or religion—that is merely one of the more noticeable and evil outcroppings of this undistinguished emotion.

Prejudice shows up in many ways, all indicating flaws in the structure of a personality. It indicates ignorance, fear of new things, inability to meet the challenge of the unknown. It woefully indicates a lack of the spirit of adventure, a lack of eagerness for knowledge of things that are new, strange, or different.

Those who are unhappily bound by prejudices can deprive themselves of many things—new foods, new restaurants, new books, new plays. Think of the hue and cry there has been against new music over the years—the prejudice against Brahms, Offenbach, Wagner because their music was "different." The alarm at the contemporary furniture designs that first came out of the Scandinavian countries, the horror at the first structures in the current style of modern architecture most people now admire so much!

You shouldn't confuse prejudice with your likes and dislikes, or with your right and privilege to be who you are and to make your own selection of your friends, your groups, your church, your political party, your clubs. Prejudice arises not from having a preference but from denying others the right and privilege to be who they are and to make their own selection of friends, groups, and so on.

All club membership, for example, on every level is by exclusion. Certainly, no group is large enough to have everyone join even if the *only* requirement were that each member have the same religion, nationality, or race.

How can you recognize—and stop—prejudice in yourself? Well—prejudice is something you can hear! And what you hear is a slurring remark, a sweeping condemnation, a broad statement of dislike. Some of the examples of vulgar prejudice sound like this: "I can't stand modern art." "Oh, she's one of those Mixolydians. They're all alike. I don't trust them." "See the *Tales of Hoffmann?* No, thank you, I think opera is silly." "Ask Maria? I think her family is foreign

120

or something. Let's not." "The Modern Dance Festival? I don't think I'd like it. I understand it's just a lot of gymnastics." "Go to the Overseas Restaurant? Really, I don't think I could eat all that queer food."

It doesn't sound like a well-bred person with broad interests and experience and a fascinating personality, does it?

When you hear yourself make a comment that is prejudiced, try to find time—very soon—to learn something about the person, the nationality, the religion, the activity that you were slurring. You will not only increase your knowledge and understanding but you will also learn how childish and insular prejudiced statements sound.

And you will start trying—in the nicest way possible—to put down any such comments you hear from others. Your response may sometimes be silence, more often a gentle "I'm afraid I can't agree with you. The Mixolydians are a splendid people and they've contributed a great deal to our culture. Have you seen the exhibit of Mixolydian art at the museum?" Or, "I thought that, too, until I had the opportunity to go to a showing of contemporary paintings." Or, "Really, I wonder if you know that Maria's mother makes the most beautiful lingerie for the Jolie Madame Shop? There are five children in the family, one of the boys has just won a scholarship to medical school, and the other four—including Maria—all help out by working after school. I think Maria is very worth knowing."

You'll think of better, more appropriate answers than these, but the basis for your answer should be a constructive, politely informative one, rather than a vehement "Don't be so prejudiced!"—although I admit there are occasions when that seems to be the only way to get through to a stubborn person.

It is an asset to your personality if you develop the habit of studying the motivations behind certain actions in which people indulge. Say you are the butt of someone's prejudice. And the person (or persons) lets you know just what his feelings are. How you react makes all the difference in the world to you personally and to the offenders. If you can practice the Bible's advice and turn the other cheek, you not only gain self-esteem, but you display a superior personality. In action, you show you are sorry for the other person—you pity him for his uninformed and very poor manners. You distinguish yourself by the dignity and forgiveness you display in not sinking to the level of the offenders. One person or one group cannot sustain an open argument or a hostile conversation. That takes two, as you know.

The *majority* of the majority always comes forward to protect and defend minority groups in today's enlightened world. Most people are good and have good instincts. What about those who don't? Take the case of a rabble rouser. Think for a moment, what is he trying to gain? It is usually a selfish motive and concludes with eventual self-destruction.

You know that prejudice indicates a lack of judgment and maturity on the part of others, a weakness in their personalities, fear and ignorance. Fine; that's very philosophical—but it doesn't help the hurt any.

The reason for your being the object of prejudice can be far from anything so obviously vulgar and foolish as your race or religion. The reason may be simply that you are a newcomer to a summer place or in a new neighborhood or a new town, and you do not yet belong and are therefore "different." Or you go to a new school where your classmates come from a different social background—higher or lower, it makes no difference; *you* are not a member of the safe, comfortable norm they know. Perhaps your family has experienced a change of fortune—your father is promoted, your mother decides to go back to work, your brother or sister or aunt or uncle takes a job or a spouse not acceptable to the people you know. Or perhaps you are a member of a minority group and find yourself excluded from activities because of accepted facets of local custom.

How do you work your way out of a box like this? Time—so hard a palliative word for a young person to take—will mend all. Time will help the others grow up, it may take you to a new neighborhood or new school. Time will make you seem less different and more of an accepted part of the group. But in the *meantime* . . . ? You can enjoy your family, enjoy new interests in books, hobbies, and other activities. You can conduct yourself so well, have so charming a manner and such pleasant manners, that the prejudiced will want to know you and will forget their preconceived ideas. And you can forget your own temporary unhappiness by giving happiness to others— working as a volunteer in a hospital, helping in a well-baby clinic, or leading play and craft activities at some community project for young children or for people who are hospitalized.

Become an ambassador for your creed or color, if one of these is the reasons you have felt prejudice, to prove to yourself and to those who have offended you that you are a better human being than those who hurt others. Make your actions admirable, and you go from an average person to one of distinction. You, individually, have defeated bigoted generalities.

The saddest thing about being the object of prejudice is that sometimes it can make you feel sorry for what you are or those you love. The destructive opinion of any prejudiced person or prejudiced group should make you all the more fiercely proud of yourself and those you love. You know all the good things about you and yours. All you know about those who are attempting to shatter your self-esteem—your *self-pride*—is that they are people who are rather shabby, self-opinionated, and snobbish. Perhaps not even worth worrying about.

The real reason most of our ancestors came to this country was that it was a young land, full of challenge and opportunity, without the shackles of prejudice, bias, and the narrow outlook of the countries they knew. You, the young in spirit and in years, have no place in your hearts for prejudice against anybody or anything. It's a big world you're going out into, and you need an open mind and an open heart to take advantage of all the friendships, knowledge, and beauty that await you.

Let's see what prejudice could cost you in just one area. Here's a list of foods that are popular in our country. Can you tell the nationality of the housewife who would prepare each of these treats?

1.	pizza pie	a.———	Japanese
2.	curry of lamb	b.———	English
3.	frankfurters and sauerkraut	c.———	Scottish
4.	beef stew	d.———	East Indian
5.	onion soup	e.———	Hungarian
6.	shortbread	f.———	Chinese
7.	sukiyaki	g.———	French
8.	goulash	h.———	German
9.	almond cookies	i.———	Irish
10.	apple tart	j.———	Italian

The right team of answers reads like this:

a-7; b-10; c-6; d-2; e-8; f-9; g-5; h-3; i-4; j-1

5. *Parties for Girls*

EATING TOGETHER has been a way of expressing friendship since man's earliest memories. As an expression of good will, tribesmen and their families would gather to "break bread together"; and after participating in bread-breaking festivities, a tribe could be counted on for loyalty and a common interest in the well-being of all those who gathered together.

Our custom of entertaining friends has descended from this simple ritual and we express our friendship and hospitality to guests in the care we take to prepare for their arrival. Planning parties is one of the most pleasant of occupations. The party you have in mind may be simply for the purpose of breaking bread—a lunch, tea, or supper; or it may be in honor of a friend who has become engaged or has just been graduated from school or your aunt who is having a baby. Sometimes you will have special-occasion parties for some seasonal event like Halloween or Valentine's Day or a carol sing at Christmas.

And sometimes you will have special-event parties. These range widely, depending on your friends' interests of the moment. The pajama party and the bridge-canasta party are great favorites. Others include the costume party—"Come as your favorite character in history" or "Come as the heroine of your favorite novel." Or the singsong, for which your main obligation (other than food) is to provide record or piano music and the words for any new songs your guests might not know.

If your guests are all busy making socks for the men in their lives, or knitting sweaters or baby presents, you might plan a woolly bee. Or you could have an afghan hook and, in one afternoon, make all the squares you'd need for an afghan to give to a charity fair.

In fact, the idea of combining church and civic duties with a pleasant lunch is one you will find very rewarding. Think of the things you might do—make dozens of boxes of brownies or cookies to sell; mend a big collection of broken toys to give to poor children; make baby layettes to be sold at the church bazaar; pool your ideas for raising money for a needy charity and then organize a plan of action.

Once the theme of the party is set, you'll want to start thinking about the girls you will invite, unless it's a committee or a club meeting. First, decide whether you're planning a sit-down lunch outside, on the porch, or at your dining table—how many will your table seat comfortably? Or if you plan a buffet lunch or supper, how many guests can you accommodate in comfort?

Then start your list by putting down the names of house guests, sisters, or cousins who will be present. Add to the list the names of the girls you most want to entertain and those who have entertained you and whom you owe. Look the list over to be sure you all have enough interests in common to insure a successful party.

When your list is set, and the time and day, you will issue your invitations—usually one to two weeks in advance of the party. These can be telephoned, written on visiting cards, if you have them, or on writing paper. This is how the invitations, acceptances, or regrets would be worded:

BY TELEPHONE:

"Hello, Janet, this is Katherine. Will you come to lunch Saturday, the tenth, at one o'clock? I'm planning a kitchen shower for Melissa Brown."

"I'd love to, Katherine. Thank you for asking me. That's Saturday, the tenth, at one."

"Wonderful, Janet, I'm so glad you can come."

or

"I'm so sorry, Katherine. We're going to visit my grandmother in Shaker Hills that weekend."

"Oh, Janet—we'll miss you! Have a good time at your grandmother's."

BY CARD:

> Kitchen shower for
> Miss Melissa Brown
>
> *Miss Katharine Bruce MacBurney*
>
> Saturday April 10ᵗʰ at 1
> R.S.V.P.

> With pleasure!
> Saturday April 10ᵗʰ at 1.
>
> *Miss Janet Barry*

or

> With many regrets
> for Saturday April 10ᵗʰ at 1-
>
> *Miss Janet Barry*

128

BY LETTER:

Dear Janet:
    Will you come
to lunch and a kitchen
shower for Melissa Brown
on Saturday the tenth at
one o'clock ?
            Looking forward
To seeing you —
            Affectionately
                Katherine

Dear Katherine:

Thank you so
much for asking me to your
lunch and shower for
Melissa on Saturday the
10th at one o'clock.

It will be such
fun to be there.

Fondly,

Janet

or

Dear Katherine:

        I'm so sorry
I can't be with you on the
10th. We're going to visit
my grandmother in Shaker
Hills that week-end.
        With best thanks
for asking me,
        Fondly,
        Janet

You've probably observed that the invitation and acceptance both give the day, date, and time. The reason for this is to be sure that each person is thinking about the *same* day, the *same* date, and the *same* time.

If you are in your very early teens and are asking friends to spend the night, too—at a pajama party, for example—you may want to ask your mother to invite your friends; that will depend in some measure on what the practice is where you live and on the size of the town where you live and how well your families know each other.

The next step is to plan the party menu. Try to think of the food preferences of your guests and, avoiding any specific things they dis-

131

like, balance the menu to include delicious and satisfying recipes. It is wise to keep the menu to a few courses, letting each dish reflect care and attention. The meal is often the high spot of the occasion, and your thought and preparation reveal a lot about you as an individual. Set your table attractively, perhaps selecting a theme if the party is for a special event or special occasion. If it's a football celebration, you might accent the table and room with the team's colors and with fall flowers. A shower might have a centerpiece of bachelor's buttons and doll-size cooking utensils. A baby shower might have a doll cradle filled with babies'-breath and sweetheart roses—or a circle of tiny dolls around a basket of daisies. You'll find many table-trimming ideas in your favorite magazines, and you might want to make a party notebook of centerpieces, menus, and recipes.

Parties for girls are fun and help you build a warm circle of friends and a very pleasant social life. The more you entertain now, the better you are fitting yourself to take your eventual place as a wife and mother, one of whose many welcome duties is entertaining for her husband and family.

Ideas for planning parties, menus, recipes, and diagrams for setting your table for sit-down meals, buffets, teas, and snack parties are in a special chapter at the end of the book, since you will use them for your parties for girls and for the parties for boys and girls which we'll discuss in the next section.

6. *When You Go Visiting*

O NE SURE SIGN you are becoming an adult is when you start visiting friends for weekends, house parties, or longer visits during vacations. You are almost sure to have a wonderful time, take up new interests, make new friends, and come home with a sense of exhilaration and a whole new outlook on life. So your first visit is quite momentous!

You may be invited by telephone but, more likely, one morning a letter will arrive that reads like this:

Dear Betsy:

Will you come for the weekend of the Essex Club dance? Bob thought he could bring you out with him on the four-thirty train on Friday, the sixth—aren't brothers convenient! The dance, Saturday, will be formal, but the rest of the weekend will be very lazy with some tennis and swimming and most meals done outside on the grill. If you can stay Sunday night, Bob can go in with you early Monday and that way you won't have any struggle with bags, etc.

Mother sends your family her love, and we are all longing to see you.

Fondly,
Sally

After reading the letter to your mother and anyone else who will listen, you write back:

Dear Sally,

How wonderful! I'll be at the Information Booth at four - twenty on the sixth. I'm so excited about the week-end I'll probably get to the station a day early, but I'll wait.

Mother says I may stay through Sunday and come in with Bob on the train Monday morning. She sends much love and so do I.

Until the sixth -

Affectionately,

Betsy

Now you will probably want to make a list of the clothes you will take, and I think one of the better ways to plan a traveling wardrobe is to list each activity and the clothes needed. That way you are fairly sure of not arriving with all your tennis equipment *except* your sneakers. And while you can always borrow things from your hostess, you are a better guest when you come with the clothes that are essential and your personal toilet articles. You will, of course, need slippers and a robe, and also a terry robe or shirt of some kind to wear after your swim.

Once your clothes are planned, you think about some small gifts to take Sally and her mother: books, candy, edibles of various kinds, records, or something in the line of special hobbies you know Sally and her mother enjoy—like collecting pitchers or little china animals. Whatever you bring need not be expensive, but it should indicate that you have made a thoughtful purchase—and pretty wrapping will help make it look so!

You meet Bob at the station with time to spare, so he is not obliged to career down the stairs lugging your two small suitcases, his brief case, and the evening papers. On the train you take your cue from Bob—if he wants to read the paper, you read, too. Many people actually dislike talking on commuting trains, and those with exacting jobs often need a few minutes to unwind after a busy day.

If, by any chance, your plans or Bob's have changed, you let your hostess know what train or bus you will take; and she will indicate whether she will meet you at the station or whether you will need to take a cab to the house. In any case, be sure she knows your exact plans however they may shift.

When you arrive, Sally and her mother will show you your room after a few minutes' preliminary chatting and they will probably ask if you would like a bath before dinner or if you want to meet on the porch when you've changed. Sally may or may not stay with you while you unpack—depending on what tasks she still has to complete—but in any case you hang up your clothes, put things in drawers, and set out your gifts to take downstairs after you've changed. Sally or her mother has probably shown you which bath to use and where the towels you will use are hung. If they haven't and you are in doubt, go and ask. Always ask when you are a guest in doubt; it's much easier for everyone and also gives your hostess the nice comfortable feeling that you are at home in her house. If you share your hostess's bedroom, she will have provided space in her closet for you and a drawer for your other belongings.

After you've changed and your room and you look reasonably neat after the flurry of unpacking, join the family and present your gifts. If your hostess has remained with you while you unpack, give her the package you've brought for her. Your hostesses may or may not unwrap your gifts the very minute they receive them, but they will be sure to before you go and to tell you how much they appreciate them. And you will be sure to look pleased and say, "I'm so glad you like the book. Mother thought you would like it." Or, "We had such fun together at the concert that I couldn't resist bringing you some of the Viennese music."

Now the visit really begins and you have two responsibilities until you get home: one is to be enchanted with every activity and every meal planned for you; the other is to fit into the schedule of the house as easily as you can. Here are some of the things you do to fit into the household routine:

- Make your bed unless your hostess tells you not to—before breakfast if you have time, or soon after.

- Set your alarm so you will arrive at breakfast on time. No alarm?— then ask Sally if she will wake you up.

- If you are sharing a bathroom with other members of the family, ask what time would be most convenient for you to take your bath. And if you're in a country house, remember the hot-water supply is often limited.

- Go to bed when Sally does, even though you're wide-awake and sit up and read till you feel sleepy.
- Ask Sally to let you help, and be alert to the times when you can help tear the salad or carry dishes out to the porch or back to the dishwasher.

Leaving after a visit—particularly when you leave on a Monday morning—is often a touch hectic. If you can, do most of your packing the night before you leave. The night before you leave is also a good time to ask your hostess if she would like you to make or change your bed; chances are she will tell you just to leave it, but occasionally she will have an appointment in town and would be grateful for the opportunity to tell you to make it up—particularly if she will be gone all day and your room is at the head of the stairs. So leave your room as neat as possible, and leave your towels and washcloth neatly folded and hung in the bathroom.

Sally's may be the kind of home where there are household employees who have served you. If so, thank them graciously before you leave and, unless your hostess has indicated otherwise, you may want to give the maid a modest tip if you have stayed more than one night. One dollar is customary for a weekend, two dollars for a week or more. Give Anna or Mary, or whomever, the tip just before you leave—with a pleasant handshake and your brief thanks for any special kindness shown you.

Within a day or two of your visit you will want to write two bread-and-butter letters—one to Sally and one to her mother. Your letters will read something like this:

Dear Mrs. Murray:

I can't thank you enough for the marvelous visit. Truly, it was one of the high spots of my whole life, and I don't think anyone could have so many perfect days in a row.

I hope when Sally comes to us in the fall we can show her half as wonderful a time!

With all my best thanks,

Devotedly,
Betsy

and to Sally:

Dear Sally:

I had the most heavenly time; and I think your family, house, and friends are superb. Even to a nice brother to take and fetch me! The dance was blissful, but then so was every minute of the whole visit.

My mother is exuberant with my plans for your visit to us this fall—but then, I have so much to live up to!

With much love to all,

Always,
Betsy

As you can tell, to be a perfect guest you need boundless good nature, enthusiasm, and appreciation. If you have these, you can look forward to a long, varied, and thoroughly enjoyable life of visiting your friends, and, in turn, having them visit you.

*Getting Along
With Boys*

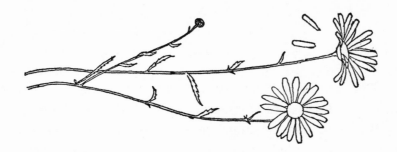

1. *The Beginnings of Love*

LOVE is the book of each life and its many chapters tell the story of a richly unfolding personality. Starting with the infant's love for his mother's tender care—the child's love for parents, family, friends, and pets; the older child's beginning love of God; the adolescent's love of love and then of a special person; the married couple's love for each other and for their children; the mature person's love for mankind; and the culminating devotion of grandparents for grandchildren—the quality of each chapter and the fineness of each relationship build a book of life that can be memorable or mediocre, warm or threadbare. Love requires care, attention, devotion, and discrimination; and it is worth all the effort you will need to put forth if you are to have love. For, if you've known any people without love in their lives, you have seen how sad and purposeless such a life can be.

There is a story told over and over in medical circles of an orphanage in Mexico where, because of a local catastrophe, hundreds of small babies were left without parents or relatives to bring them up. They were, of necessity, placed in an orphanage and there were so few people on the staff that, overworked as they were, they had no time to give the babies anything except the most basic care. No time for the loving play, crooning, cuddling, and general admiration a baby requires to exist. Few of the infants lived very long, despite adequate food and medical care. They literally starved to death—starved not for food but for love.

And a life lived without love is starved, too. You need the whole of love to have a full and happy life. If you appreciate this, you will make each chapter a fine one that you can remember happily—knowing that you gained and grew in love at each phase. Not that each relationship will be a perfect one. It won't, because you, an imperfect human being, are dealing with imperfect human beings. But if, in the imperfect relationships, you can know that you did your best and that you gained and grew, your memories can give you pleasure.

There is a lovely inscription for a sundial that Henry van Dyke wrote early in this century:

> Hours fly, flowers die.
> New days, new ways
> Pass by. Love stays.

And love does stay, if you make it welcome, coloring and warming the chapters of your life.

Falling in love with love

In this book of young living, our main concern on the subject of love is its beginnings—the boy-and-girl relationship that will, in the years to come, bring you to a contented marriage. Just at what age you will start falling in love is difficult to tell. Each girl matures at her own speed; so you may be thirteen, seventeen, or twenty-five before you experience the bliss and confusion of falling in love. And most of the confusion arises from the fact that you are falling in love with love, not really with a person. The boy next door who's been a good friend for ten years suddenly becomes a mysterious, glamorous being composed of one third Lancelot, one sixth your favorite movie star, one third your favorite singer, and one sixth an ideal man you've been building up in your mind all your life. He ceases to exist as a person for you, and your pleasant friendship ceases to exist temporarily. This is the reason you sigh and blush, become tongue-tied when you try to talk to him, sit dreaming over a souvenir that means *him*, and, in general, are miserably happy. He doesn't understand this any more than you do and, because he probably hasn't reached the stage of being in love with love or a girl yet, he is equally confused, not happy about the whole situation, and will take refuge in purely masculine activities that exclude girls.

At this stage of your life, you will do well to spend your time with girls who have brothers and beaux milling about their houses rather than waiting at home for the elusive Steve to telephone or come by to see you. More likely than not, he is avoiding you like the plague and you are depriving yourself of fun and friends and also the chance of seeing other boys and, subconsciously, learning about the way they think and react and about their likes and dislikes.

How to meet boys

"How did you meet?" is the classic question in all romances. If you have a big family with older sisters and brothers, your chances of meeting boys at home are fairly good. But your best bet is to enjoy an active, interested life at school and in your community. It is true that Robert Browning fell in love with the housebound Elizabeth

Barrett, but neither you nor I may ever see their like again. If you are a bubbling, busy person, boys will want to know you and that is the most important part of meeting boys. You've probably heard the adults in your family observe that "any girl can get married if she wants to." Well, any girl can have beaux, too, if she wants them. But it means you have to participate in activities where there are men to meet rather than relying on your family and friends to introduce boys to you.

Where can you meet boys? Just like the girls who are fun to know because they are lively and busy, the boys you will want to know are also bustling around, members of clubs, active at games, working at part-time jobs. Your cue, then, is to learn about sports that interest men, both spectator sports like football, basketball, baseball, hockey, and so on, and active sports like swimming, tennis, golf, riding, sailing, skiing—whatever you have the chance to learn that your family can afford. The various sports magazines will also teach you the language and the news in sports so you will have a ready topic of conversation with boys you meet.

Organizations in your school, church, and community—other than the purely feminine ones—provide you with a good meeting ground, and so does taking part in church and community work. Part-time jobs, other than baby-sitting, can also bring new opportunities to meet boys.

Blind dates are the source of many magazine romances and sometimes even in real life! On the whole, most blind dates need investigating before you accept them. Who is he, who is his family, where does he go to school, how well does the girl or boy arranging the date know him, where will you go and in whose car—all are vital questions for which you should get clear answers. This is important, even when you are not interested in the date as a basis for meeting a boy but are being asked to go as a favor to a friend who needs a fourth. Double-dating is fun only when all four people have the same interests and standards; otherwise you can have an unhappy evening, per-haps be shanghaied into going places that you prefer not to—or into activities that are more adult than you are ready for.

The question of enforcing your own high moral standards looms as a problem usually because of insufficient knowledge of the people you are with or the activities planned for the evening. That is why you have a responsibility to see that at least one of your parents meets the boy you are going out with—and to be organized about telling your mother who he is, where you are going, and setting a time for your return home. If you get into situations you might be ashamed of, you will be unhappy, because, to be happy, you must have pride in yourself. You want to be a responsible individual and enjoy the respect of others.

Of course, even with the best preparation on your part, you may find the evening ending at a place you disapprove or feel your parents would disapprove. This is a situation you can handle so long as you keep your wits about you. Tears, indignant disapproval, voiced fear of what your parents would think—all are bad technique. The best approach is to appeal to your date with a thoroughly legitimate-sounding excuse for leaving. It has to be one he will be sympathetic to, whether it's a sudden violent ache in your middle, the informa-tion that your father won't get you that new tennis racket if you're not home by eleven, the fact that you're leaving for the big football weekend at your father's college and you just remembered you haven't packed and your family will skin you alive if you're not ready to leave at 6 A.M. In other words, ask his help in rescuing you from a situation other than the one you're actually in.

How to understand boys

Understanding men is a hobby that can engross you all your life. Each man is different and takes a different brand of understanding, and yet each has many of the same basic qualities that go into the making of a man. The same courage, ambition, gentleness, flashes of magnificence, impatience with petty thoughts or actions, irritability when tired, retreat into silence when worried, small-boy recklessness.

The psychiatrists tell us that a girl's relationship with her father will have a tremendous bearing on the happiness of her marriage, because more than likely she will marry a man whose personality is like her father's. So your first step in understanding men is to study your father and learn to get along with him very well indeed. Notice his likes and dislikes, his enthusiasms, the things that please him or make him laugh, the attentions that give him pleasure. Watch your mother and her skill at babying him when he's tired, waiting till the opportune time to bring up family worries, or new expenses, or the news that your puppy dug up the new geraniums your neighbor had just set out.

If you study your brothers, young uncles, and friends, and supplement your "clinical" study with books about family life—both novels and real accounts—you'll wind up with a fistful of useful "dos" and "don'ts." Read biographies of interesting men both to learn about men and their ambitions, successes, and failures, and also to learn about their wives and sweethearts, and the factors that made each a happy or unhappy relationship.

Learning women's techniques in managing males is the subject of many an all-woman discussion and also of many books you will enjoy, like Clarence Day's delicious accounts of his skillful mother in *Life with Father* and *Life with Mother*. To be skillful, a woman has to have certain basic attributes; they include loving the male involved, having a sense of humor, good taste, and common sense, and a very feminine ability to look prettily bewildered and helpless while plotting and achieving a goal she thinks is really important. You remember we were talking about saving face a while back. In dealing with any male, the art of face saving is essential. Traditionally, he is the head of the family, the dominant partner, the man in the situation.

Even on those occasions when you both know his decision is wrong, more often than not you will be wise to go along with his decision— temporarily—until you can find a face-saving solution.

And if it's a situation that needs immediate action, you can always retreat into a feminine corner by saying you're sure he's right but would he be kind enough to go along with you at least until you've had a chance to think it over. (You may think it over and, in a calmer moment, discover he is right after all!)

Falling in love with one man

Suddenly the day will arrive when you realize you have fallen in love not with an ideal of love but with one special boy. You are sure this is the great romance of your life, that he is the only man in the world for you; and if he doesn't love you in return, take you to the spring dance, and marry you, you will wither away.

To any girl with a heart, each love seems like the real thing—"I'm really in love for the first time" has probably been said almost as many times as "I love you!" If there were an easy answer to the question of whether a love is real or synthetic, it would have been discovered thousands of years ago.

Time will tell. You may really be in love, and the boy may have only a friendly affection for you. In every family there are those truly happy couples who literally fell in love at first sight, married, and lived happily ever after. I've known them, perhaps you already know a few. While this is a romantic and exciting beginning to a marriage, it isn't necessary for an equally enriching love. Time may turn the boy with only a friendly affection into a man who loves you deeply. Time may diminish the great love you thought you had for him. And time may bring you the man who satisfies your more adult needs and goals a thousand times better than the one you loved at seventeen.

In the meantime, you learn that getting along with a man you love—and who loves you—requires a great deal more talent, heart, and wit than merely walking hand in hand into the sunset. And because the boy whose heart you hope to win is probably no more experienced at falling in love than you are, he may be very diffident about letting you know the true state of his feelings—just as you may be suddenly shy about revealing your heart to him. And you now will be living through your first taste of the gambit stage with its fragile decisions that can make this, your first romance, a happy or a sad one.

The first decision you need to make is to be yourself—not your aunt, your mother, your sister, the heroine of the last movie you've seen. *Yourself*. That's why the boy has shown an interest in you. If you have been the healthy, freckled girl who was fun to play tennis or to ski with, to take on picnics or bird watching, you can't turn into a dreamy, poetry-reading-by-an-open-fire girl and expect your young man to be anything but bewildered. Don't give up the poetry. Take it with you to read in front of the fire at the ski lodge or at the picnic spot.

And the second decision you need to make is to be honest with the boy. Tell him what's on your mind. If you disagree with him, if you're disappointed in something he has or hasn't done, if you misunderstand about a date, if you think he should take you and not someone else to the dance—find an opportunity to discuss the situation with him in as frank and friendly a manner as you can. He may be the most charming, brilliant boy in the world, but he can't read your mind or analyze what's troubling you. Men, as you will learn, dislike unpleasantness; if your beau feels there is a heavy air of unexplained trouble, he may prefer to wander away rather than probe the cause of the unpleasantness. But if you are honest and good-tempered with him, you two will probably build a better relationship through solving the difficulties that are bothering you.

You will have other decisions of procedure to make. Will you confine your dates to him, and if you do, is this agreeable to your family

150

and to his? Or can you make a compromise arrangement, making a steady date for Saturday nights, with the rest spontaneous? What do you plan to do about always being available when he calls—particularly if he is the casual type who waits till seven-thirty to call? (I suspect that, if you are always available, you are not enjoying enough activity in clubs, community work, and with the girls you know.) When will you call him? This would be a good time to make a firm rule never to call any man—beau, fiancé, husband—without a definite reason and to make the call as brief and pleasant as possible. You can call to invite him to a party, you can call about changing arrangements you've made for a party, about a club or committee meeting, for a brief chat if he's ill. You can even call him on his birthday if he's out of town—but briefly! If you've ever watched your brother's grimaces when he's been haunted by telephone calls from a love-smitten young lady, you would better understand the embarrassment the boy suffers and the blow you are dealing your relationship by being aggressive.

Most of your dates will be suggested and planned by the boy. But you will do your share of entertaining your friends, and he will naturally be invited to these parties. Your mother will probably encourage you to bring him home for lunch after church, or to stay for supper some evenings. Now and then you may be given tickets to a concert or play, and you can invite him to that. Perhaps your family belongs to a club, and you can occasionally invite him to play tennis and have lunch. But, on the whole, *most* of the invitations should come from him.

Being pleasing instead of pesky to each other's families is a big part of the public-relations side of any romance. You each love your family and appreciate the comfort of their approval. And when your family likes and approves the one you love, it makes all the relationships of your life mesh like a well-tempered precision instrument. Not like hammer and tongs!

151

By public relations I mean the basic things, like telling your family about the boy before you introduce him to them, not hustling him out of the house but giving him and your parents a chance to talk to each other now and then. Asking your family to invite him to an occasional family meal. Getting him to work with a softball team for underprivileged boys, collecting the books for the community fair, helping you carry the ten boxes of butter cookies to the church bazaar—you know, the efforts that will please them.

And you should encourage your beau to try to build the same relationship for you with his family. You don't want to spend all your time with each other's families (nor do they want you to, I'm sure); but every now and then it is necessary, in building a happy life, to spend some time with the senior members of the clan—or in doing something for them. One way you can endear yourself to a boy's mother is by offering to take care of a young brother or sister—your beau's mother can't get much help from him alone in this respect, but with you to help she might be able to get to a meeting or the hairdresser or to a matinee that she might otherwise miss. You can help plan projects for the young—a trip to the zoo, the museum, a movie, a picnic, a ball game—and you will be endearing yourself and your beau to everyone in his family. If he has a strong family feeling, as so many men do, you will also be increasing your own rating.

Girls and boys sometimes get tongue-tied when talking to grown-ups, particularly when it's the family involved. Whether it's a casual meeting or a dinner party, your beau's mother or his favorite uncle—whether it's any adult, actually—a girl's best conversational friend is polite interest in the other person, his business, hobbies, interests, opinions. If you know what they are, you can say, "Steve tells me you're a very enthusiastic fisherman, Mr. Blaine. What kind of fishing do you do?" Or, "I heard about your plan to beautify the South Street area, Mr. Purdy. Do you think it will take long to achieve?" Or, "Did it take you a long time to develop your plan?" Or, "Are

152

you and Steve's father in the same line of business, Mr. Stark?" Or, "Steve's father and my uncle played three sets of tennis this morning. They had a very close match. Do you have a favorite sport, Mrs. Carter?"

Your interest in Steve's family and in their friends will make you an ever more welcome member of their family group. I have even known girls who remained on the warmest of terms with a boy's family years after the boy and girl had lost all romantic interest in each other. You may lose your heart and then find it again—but there's no reason why you shouldn't gain both wisdom and friends in the process.

In addition to its pleasures, love has its problems. Your family—and his—will enjoy your romance but they will deprecate the time you devote to it, particularly if you slough off the family activities and the help you formerly contributed to the running of the house. If you never have time to go swimming with the family or to clean your room and press your clothes, if you are too busy to help your young sister with the costume she's making for her class play, if your school-work takes a noticeable slump, your family's indulgent pleasure at your love affair may soon cease to be indulgent. You still need to be a responsible citizen, even though in love!

Sometimes your friends can pose difficulties. Your beau may come from the next town—or from a noticeably richer or poorer section of your town. Your friends may resent him because, unless you make a real effort to include them in some of your dates with him, they may feel you are drifting away from them. Even though your new man is glamour personified, you still need to be a friend to the girls and boys next door.

Money is another poser, too. If you are going out with one boy on an exclusive basis, the temptation to offer to share expenses for movies, tennis balls, and so on will be very great. Resist it. You can let him know that you enjoy staying home and watching TV, listening to records and dancing, or playing cards. You can plan parties at your home. You can get friends to plan parties. You can suggest just going for a walk. You are entitled to help him *not* to spend his money. But trying to pay your way can only be awkward and damaging to you both.

The things you do to build a sound relationship

Love represents a sharing of experience and expression, and a happy love affair needs to represent more than fun dates and holding hands. You should make it a matter of course to go to a church together and to share in some church activities. Friends should be included in most of your plans, because you two will have a healthier, more outgoing relationship if you are part of a group. You are both part of a community, too, so some of your time should go into doing some civic and charitable work together. Each of you can provide the other with a great deal of inspiration in the many aspects of your lives.

You need also to share the general interests of your families. Perhaps your married brother and his wife and children have Sunday-afternoon ice-skating parties or picnics by the lake in summer. Ask them to invite you and your beau. It's good to gather people you love together; you get a new point of view about each of them and find new things to admire. Your brother may be delighted to give your beau just the information he's been seeking about college or a profession or a summer job.

The sum of love

Some girls and boys fall in love at sixteen, marry when they finish college—or while they're still in college—and love only each other all their lives. More often though, you will have been in and out of love a number of times before you marry. But each romance is a prepara-

154

tion for the real thing; each teaches you to be a finer, more adult person—a better friend, more worthy of love.

And because you have no way of knowing whether your first or your tenth beau may turn out to be the man you want to build your life with, you will want to handle the delicate question of love-making with spirit and wariness and judgment. If you love someone, you want to show your affection; you wouldn't be normal if you didn't. And the pleasant give-and-take of kisses, holding hands, the caressing friendly pat on the shoulder as you go by are all very much needed by you both. You—loving and being loved—build up your own value in your own eyes. You become self-confident, assured. Somebody loves you for no other reason than that you are you.

You will be wise indeed if you keep your first and all your romances on a beyond-reproach level. The major responsibility for any romance disintegrating into an affair—that can lead only to reproaches—is the girl's. Your chances of causing the boy you love, or yourself, anything but unhappiness are fairly slim if you fail to conform to the generally approved standards of behavior. More than that, you will be burdening yourself with unnecessary regrets when your real and lasting romance comes along. Your own standards are pretty well set by now, through your parents' and your church's guidance as well as by your own good sense. Better heed them.

Sometimes circumstances are such that your heart, your youth, your standards can all meet brilliantly in an early and successful marriage. Your families may have a tradition of marrying young and may be able to afford sending you both on through school. (More and more colleges have dormitories especially for married students.)

I think many adults forget the great idealism and also the great innocence of youth. One of the ideals of our civilization is the lovely innocent bride traditionally dressed in pure white and garlanded with delicate spring blossoms. Your wedding day is the zenith of your romance with the man you love; and the greatest treasure you can bring your bridegroom is your whole heart, your innocence, and your idealism still shining. No casual love-making, no transitory excitement of seeming to be sophisticated and daring, is worth the surrender of the faith, love, and truth you owe your husband.

So, unless your circumstances are so fortunate that you can and should marry the boy you love while you're still in your teens, think carefully before trading away any of the ideal beauty of your bridal day.

It isn't easy to say no to a persuasive and charming boy. If you are fond of him and he has great attraction for you, you may be afraid of losing him—especially if he makes those age-old statements that include such phrases as "You really don't care about me ..." "If you loved me as much as I love you ..." "But we love each other ..." or "You know I want to marry you. ..." Many hundreds of lines of advice have been written telling girls what to say in this situation. The only sentence worth remembering is "No, please take me home. Now." When you are safely at your door, securely away from the persuasive quiet and the moonlight, you can and should try to have a sincere and affectionate discussion of your feelings. You will indicate that he is dear to you, that you find him attractive, and that you are happy that he is interested in you; perhaps that, if you were both ready to get married, you've never met a boy you would rather have for your husband—but now, you're not ready for marriage and you don't want anything less; he's one of the best friends you have, you're not anxious to part with him, and so you hope he will go along with your point of view. He may sulk, storm away in a rage, but it's pretty certain he'll come back on your terms. Once out of the moonlight, most boys are as chary of a casual affair as you are.

One of the most important values you will receive from your early loves is the knowledge of how important friendship is to love. When you reach the stage where a man tells you that he not only loves you but, more than that, he likes you, you will know that you have passed one of the great milestones in becoming a fine woman. When you can remain friends with a man, despite differences of opinion that are both major and minor, you have built a strong, good personality.

And every romance has its differences, with the major ones often being much easier to handle than the minor ones! Flirting is probably inevitable in youth, because at this age it's almost second nature for a bright pretty girl to sparkle at the men and boys she meets. After all, she's been flirting since she learned to play peekaboo and flutter her eyelashes as a toddler, and receiving only approval from her family for being such a little darling. It is quite a lesson to learn that your young man expects you to confine your flirting to him when you're out with him.

Jealousy is the unhappy long-range end result of unchanneled flirting either on your part or on your beau's. There is truly no place for the morale-wrecking misery of jealousy in any good relationship. If you are jealous of your beau's interest in another girl—or several others —you will do well to have an honest discussion of your jealousy with him. He may really have fallen in love with another girl and still not be quite willing to break with you. You will have to decide whether you care enough to put aside your jealousy and resentment and give him a chance to make up his mind. If you don't, part now while you can still speak kindly to each other! And it may be possible that he is thoroughly confused and either laughs off any discussion or refuses to discuss the problem at all. This is the time to be surgical and make a clean break with him; if he can't communicate with you, you haven't got a friendship that is a working one. On the other hand, you may discover to your surprise that he is really not interested in the other girl but is trying shock techniques to persuade you to stop flirting, or because he has mistakenly feared you were interested in another boy—or because he needed the reassurance of knowing you cared and were upset because he seemed to like another girl better. But you won't know where you stand unless you talk it out.

Whatever the reason, breaking off a love affair is a sad experience. The ideal is to stay friends. It makes life easier for you, for your family, the boy's family, and all your circle. Sometimes the causes for the breakup seem too monumental for you ever to be able to speak to him again after the good-by speech that you rehearse with so many tears. If you can, I think you will be happier in the long run if you can avoid the luxury of the farewell scene. If you can quietly and without explanation thank him for calling you but refuse any invitation, a few such rejections will get through to him. Manlike, he may start paying you a great deal of sudden attention, because he may not believe you are serious about leaving him. If your mind is made up, stay with your decision, because the end is probably inevitable and you are in command of both yourself and the situation now. If you can part amicably, it is always possible that a few years from now you might be able to build a more satisfactory relationship. And it is equally possible that he has an older brother or cousin who will come home from school or the army and be very much attracted to you. If your ex-beau is obliged, by your good behavior and his own conscience, to say only good things about you, you will not lose out in securing an eligible new man.

Sometimes a boy just walks out of your life. He doesn't keep a date or he stops phoning with no explanation. If you realize that this is not a man's way of behaving and that he is being both immature and discourteous, you can get through the bad time better. You can't *not* be hurt by so cavalier a cavalier but, for the salvaging of your own pride, try to maintain a cool front when you do see him at school, on the street, coming out of the movies. If you are sizzling with wrath, let off steam some other way than at him. Paint your room, scrub the floor of the playroom, or follow the example of one girl I knew: she told her mother she was just about ready to explode with wrath and could she please have all the chipped and cracked china and pottery her mother was willing to part with. To her mother's and her own eventual amusement, she took it outside behind the garage, smashed it piece by piece into a big box. (Probably muttering, "All *right*, Johnny Clark, all *right*.") Then when she next saw Johnny Clark, she was able to muster up a social smile and say, "Hello, Johnny, how nice to see you."

Avoiding verbal bitterness will make life much more pleasant for you; and, instead of simmering, you can get around and about, see your friends, and acquire a new beau. If you go into a decline of misery, you will deny yourself the fun of seeing your friends; and if you spend your time discussing the woes of your broken romance with your friends, they may presently deny you the fun of seeing them.

Sometimes a broken romance is salvageable, and if you say a lot of unkind things about the boy, you may be doubly sorry when you do patch things up. Remember, the cause of the split was in some measure your fault, too; and, following the golden rule, you trust he will not say unkind things about you either.

Most romances are loving and kind in spirit, and though you may drift apart, you do so without bitterness because you are both seeking the one person whom you will love all your life. When you find the one person, you will understand the full meaning of these lines written by an Arabian poet in the long-ago thirteenth century:

> Love was before the light began.
> When light is over, love shall be.

2. *Flirting*
Fair and Square

Someday the one you love the best will come along and, in spite of all the love stories, he may be equally attracted and still fail to give you a whirlwind of attention. It may be because, like many especially attractive men, he really doesn't appreciate his own charm. And, in this competitive day when girls are fairly forthright, he may expect a more frank expression of your interest.

Overaggression is certainly unfeminine and, although you may resort to it, I don't think you'll be very comfortable. True, your friends may make lengthy phone calls to boys; do all the party plan-

160

ning and inviting; wait for them at the gym, the football or baseball field, or at the soda bar; write them long, frequent, and overly enthusiastic love letters. But, somehow, just as in business and in marriage, someone has to be the leader. And, in a man-woman relationship, I doubt whether any woman can boss a real man. Perhaps the reason so many girls are trying to take the lead is that they start dating early and that girls mature more rapidly than boys. And often the boys they should be going out with are away from home or in the service. If your overaggressive friends of, say, fifteen were interested in more mature boys, I suspect they would quickly change their not-so-pretty ways. And I also suspect that by the time the girls are a little older, they will find that changing those ways is not so easy as it would have been to forego the few extra dates that resulted from aggressiveness.

But I agree that you, like women of every era, have to let a man know you like him, are interested in him, and hope to spend more time with him. Even in the primly proper Victorian age, ladies used their delicate lace and ivory fans to flirt with gentlemen; and a whole code of messages was transcribed with turns and furls of the fan— saying, "I love you," "I hate you," "I never want to see you again," "I forgive you," "Can we meet in the solarium?" "Shall we dance?" "Can't you get our host to introduce you?" It was a very forward young miss indeed who would *say* these things, and if she did, the young man would probably not have been half so tantalized.

But then, as now, any pretty, lively girl had no intention of letting a devastating man get away if she could help it, so she developed her own methods of flirting on the square.

Today hi-fi has replaced the gramophone; punting on the river has given way to the less stately outboard; the sprigged dimity has lost out to nylon chiffon; and the sports car has outdistanced the buggy—but a girl would still like to have a man chase her until she catches him.

Here are suggestions that may help the chase:

when you see him

smile

call him by name

say something nice. "I see you have your football letter—it looks wonderful! Are you going out for a sport this winter? . . . Basketball? I *adore* basketball. We watch every game on television. What position do you play?"

or, "That was a wonderful report you made at the dance committee meeting. Especially the silk-screened posters. They sound terribly difficult . . . is it the sort of thing a girl could do?"

or, "I saw your sister at the church dance Saturday—she looked *so* pretty. We all had a wonderful time—don't you ever go to them?"

if he has never asked you out

get a friend to ask him to her house for a valid reason—a club to be formed, a committee meeting, a hot-dog roast. You will have a chance to talk to him and get to know some of his interests.

be fascinated with the subjects he's interested in. This is easier if you know something about the subjects. In any case, get him to talk by way of prodding murmurs like, "That must be *very* difficult . . . how did you learn so much about it? . . . This would make a wonderful article for my section on the school paper. . . . Would you possibly be willing to come and talk to the Sunday Evening Society about this—I'd be glad to help you with the exhibits."

without grilling him, try to learn about his interests, his hobbies, his favorite sports. If you find any you like or would like to take up, ask him where he shops for the records, what tennis courts he uses, where he studies the accordion, where he sails, swims, fishes, skis. Then you'll always know where he might be if someone suggests you go record shopping, play tennis, or whatever. You will also know what new interests you'd better develop, what to ask for on your next birthday, what tennis courts to use. You may astonish your father by asking him to teach you to fish. Once you know something about the boy, your subtle opportunities are limitless.

when he does ask you out

(and if he hasn't by now you are probably wasting your time) say you'd love to. You've wanted to see the movie—or the game —so much. Be enthusiastic about his plans for the date, remembering Mrs. Bennett's advice to her daughter in *Pride and Prejudice*: "Sparkle, Mary—but not too much!"

when he comes to get you, be ready and waiting. Introduce him with obvious pleasure to your parents.

show that you are proud to be with him by listening to what he says, deferring to his judgment about where to sit, letting him order for you at the hot-dog stand or the restaurant or the soda bar (perhaps let him choose for you, too—men love this piece of delicate flattery).

if your parents are still up when you return, ask him to have some hot chocolate or some kind of drink or snack that he can help you prepare.

thank him when he leaves, hold out your hand and say something that will send him away feeling pleased that he took you

163

out, pleased with you and very pleased with himself. "I had the most wonderful time" is not bad. "I'm so glad you asked me to the game, Jim—I loved going with you" is better. Or, "I don't think I've ever enjoyed a game so much. It must have been you!" Best of all is remembering some funny incident of the evening before you say your thank-you's.

if he hasn't made another date

wait a week or so. He may have a money problem.

ask him to join a committee you're heading for your school, church, community, or charitable work. If you're not on one, join one; or start one, with the sanction of some respected group.

if he has some special talent like fencing, golf, baseball, swimming, basketball, see if your family would get him to help your young brother. Or perhaps he has an enviable scholastic record, and could tutor your brother or sister. If he's helping your brother with sports, you can always come round to admire toward the end of the lesson. Or bring in some lemonade and cookies at the end of the tutoring session. That is, *not* always. Even if he is being a very devoted beau to you, don't always be around when he is at your house on a bona fide job. Nor, when you are there and he is working, should you be conducting a merry gathering with other boys present—especially if he might conceivably be jealous of them.

the not-too-obvious attentions

you can always phone for a real reason. If you manufacture the reason, be sure it sounds real. Real ones include an invitation to a party; an invitation from your mother to come to dinner before going to the school play; very important news about a

164

friend; details about a committee meeting; a request for help on a school, church, community project; a quite honest admission of not being quite sure where or when you were to meet for a date he has made or a meeting he is taking you to. In every instance you should identify yourself when you call ("Hello, this is Jane Harrington. May I speak to Steve, please?"), so your call is out in the open. You should be cheery, state the reason for your call, get the facts, and then, before you quickly hang up, say something nice, like "I'm glad I had a good excuse to call. It's nice to talk to you. Good-by, Steve." Or, "I did have the most marvelous time at the Blakes'. You're probably the best beau in all Fairfield." Something pleasant, fairly personal, so he will know you were glad to talk to him as well as being rather required to make the call.

you *can* write to him, even when you're both in town. You can send a clip from the paper on a subject dear to his heart—or a clip about him or his family or a friend. You can even send him a clip about you or some committee you're on. With it, you scribble a sentence or two, add a funny drawing if you enjoy that, and sign it "Fondly," "Devotedly," "Best always," "XXX," or whatever the current closing is among your friends.

there is no particular point in your writing longer letters to him unless he is out of town, but if everyone else is writing letters you certainly can answer those he writes to you. One thing about letters—they should be friendly, sweet, sincere, affectionate; but in no case should they sound as though they were written by a script writer for a very adult movie or by someone overaffected with Sanskrit love poetry. The boy will treasure the letter more if it represents you, not your idea of a glamorous love letter.

of course, if he has some tremendous personal victory—being elected captain of a team, president of the class or club, winning a special prize, you can write a note of congratulation. And if he is ill, you should write and keep him posted with the news and also your interest in him.

if he asks for your photograph, you'll give him one. If he wants you to write a message on it, make it a simple one in the event that he might want to put it up in his room. Your message should be one that indicates you like him—but it shouldn't make him the object of unnecessary teasing. You can always write, "To Steve. Affectionately, Janie." Or, "For dear Steve from Jane." Or, "Jane to Stephen, with love. April, 1957." Or if he has been captain of a team, president of the class, or the lawyer in the school play, you can make some reference to his "title."

if he likes handmade socks, you can volunteer to make some for him. He will derive untold pleasure both from watching you knit them and from wearing them and telling others that you made them for him.

However you choose to flirt with him, make it an honest kind of attention, based on the premise that you like him and want him to like you. Just collecting boys and then discarding them is unthrifty of you and deeply unkind to the boys. When you flirt with one boy to attract and hold his interest, that flirtation is fair and square.

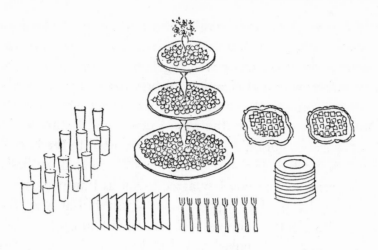

3. *Parties for Boys and Girls*

ENTERTAINING boys and girls is, in large measure, the basis for the major part of the social life you will enjoy as an adult—and it is one of the most exciting aspects of your teen years. You learn early that the most expensive and elegant of parties—planned to be expensive and elegant, with no particular interest in the likes and dislikes of the guests—can be a dismal failure, while a very modest party—planned with affection and interest for the guests' pleasure—can be a memorable evening for every one lucky enough to be invited.

What makes a party fun? If you and the people you invite are brimming with enthusiasm, eager to have a delightful time, to laugh and to be pleased with one another, the party is sure to be a success. That means that you will need to be a good planner—inviting boys and girls who will get along well together, having all the details of cooking and serving and cleaning up organized in your mind—and, if necessary, on paper!—so that the mechanics of the party run smoothly. It means having the record player and the records ready, having the games not only planned but entrusted to the best games-man you've invited. If you're going on to a football or basketball game, it means having one boy agree to act as transportation chair-man, taking charge of who goes in whose car and at what time. It means having plenty of simple, delicious food that can, for the most part, be prepared and cooked ahead of time on the theory that it's always nice if you can attend your own party!

Why are some parties *not* fun? If the hostess is harried and obvi-ously running around in disorganized circles, the party loses some of its savor for the guests. If the hostess is all too apparently having a great quarrel with her beau—who is acting as the host for the eve-ning—the gaiety of the evening is certain to be quenched. If plans are poorly made and everyone is anxious about getting to the game on time, spontaneity is lost. If, to sum it up, the proper theme for every party—that of giving pleasure to friends—is not the main thought of the hostess, the chances for the party being fun are slim indeed.

In planning a party for boys and girls, your first decision is the reason for the party's being at all; once that point is settled, the rest of your plans will fall into line. I find that, for teen-agers, parties tend to divide into three main types. First, the at-home party that ranges from a cook-out on the back-yard barbecue; to an afternoon or evening of dancing, listening to records; to a supper party. Then, the at-home-and-abroad parties that either begin with lunch or supper at your house before you go to a football or basketball game, ice skating or swimming, or to a dance; or end at your house for lunch, brunch, or supper after one of those events. And third, the rarer occasions when you entertain away from home—perhaps at a small dance your parents or grandparents give, or lunch at a restaurant or a club before a special movie or sports event, or a civic or charitable event for which your family takes seats or a table.

With the reason for the party determined and an amiable group of guests decided on, you will next invite your guests. By this time you are quite knowledgeable in the art of issuing invitations, but since boys are involved in these parties, it might be wise to remember that written invitations to men are practical and thoughtful—they then have both a reminder and a handy reference for such details as time, place, and the kind of clothes they will be expected to wear.

Pre-party planning, menus, and recipes for many kinds of parties are given in a chapter at the end of the book, but there are a few special notes that especially apply to parties for boys and girls.

First of these is the question of a chaperone. Your parents will probably mastermind this situation for you, but if for any reason they can't be at home for your party, do ask another married couple —either in your family or in one of your friends'—to come and stay until your party is over. They don't need to—and they won't—stay right with your group; more likely they'll be watching television or playing cards or reading in another room. But they'll be there.

Introductions are your responsibility as the hostess. If all the boys and girls know each other, then you have only to introduce them to your parents or to the other adults who are at your home. Remember, you always present the younger person to the older ones, the boy to the girl, the student to the teacher. Introductions narrow down to these situations:

- Boy meets girl   "Mary, this is Johnny Clark. Mary Moore, John."
- Boy meets boy   "This is Johnny Clark. Howard Brown."

169

- Girl meets girl   "Mary, this is Anne Bryan—Anne, Mary Moore."

- Boy meets parents   "Mother, this is Johnny Clark."
"Daddy, this is Johnny Clark."

- Girl meets parents   "Mother, this is Anne Bryan."
"Anne, this is my father."

And if you think there can be any possible confusion in the last name of the adult—if your mother has remarried or if you have a stepfather—you add the name in this fashion:

"This is Johnny Clark. My mother, Mrs. Laine."
"This is Johnny Clark. My stepfather, Mr. Laine."

- Boy meets chaperones   "This is Johnny Clark. Mrs. Higgins."
"Mr. Higgins, this is Johnny Clark."

- Girl meets chaperones   "Mrs. Higgins, this is Anne Bryan."
"Anne, this is Mr. Higgins."

Both Anne Bryan and Johnny Clark should rise to met your mother or Mrs. Higgins; Johnny Clark should rise to meet your father or Mr. Higgins. It is always a nice gesture for girls to rise when meeting adults, but it is not necessary on most occasions. It is, however, a mark of respect, and reveals a genuinely gracious manner.

Just for fun   One of the happiest aspects of growing up is the joy of learning to be a good hostess at parties for mixed groups of girls and boys. Successful party givers usually rely on a few tried-and-true rules that make less work for the hostess and ensure more fun for the guests. At the end of this book, in a special section, you will find a bounty of how-to's for giving successful parties, and among them are many ideas for popular parties to give for boys and girls. You will find party themes, menus, recipes, decorating and game ideas in The Party Notebook.

Becoming an Adult

1. *Getting Along With Grownups*

EARLY in this century, the people who expound on child raising confidently advised that the young were expected to do as they were told and to be seen but not heard. Along in the twenties, a new theory called "progressive education" came along; its tenets of unshackling the young allowed children unlimited freedom of thought, word, and deed. Indeed, those parents and teachers who were real devotees of early progressive education seemed to have only one rather cowed protest which was something along the lines of "Tolerate adult attitudes—someday you'll be one, too."

Fortunately, theories come and theories go; and most parents, happily engrossed in busy, enjoyable activities with their children, go right ahead using their common sense and doing the very best they can in their judgment. Neither parents nor children are always going to agree with each other—that's just another theory that looks very nice on paper—and your parents' hopes won't really focus for you, until you, too, become a parent.

The richness of family life—where pleasures and obligations must be shared for all to benefit—is one of the greatest blessings you will receive on earth. Like all treasures, it must be counted, shined, and polished, kept in use for all to see and enjoy.

Traditionally and emotionally, boys and their mothers, and girls and their fathers, have a closer bond than fathers and sons and mothers and daughters. This is reasonable by nature, because, to a great extent, the parent of the opposite sex will be the one who sets the child's pattern of relationship with that sex. In most families, however, this moderate favoritism is outweighed by the wealth of affection each member of the family has for the other.

A girl's comradeship with her father has been discussed in "The Beginnings of Love"; but, so far, we've said very little about that paramount devotion, love, and sympathy of interests that only a mother and daughter can know. It has been said that it takes the genius of an Einstein to be a perfect mother, and most mothers have that kind of genius to a great degree. Think for a moment of the many people your mother has to be to you: a friend, an older sister, a mother. To your brother: a friend, a big sister, an older girl, a mother. To your father: a sweetheart, wife, mother, friend, little girl, housekeeper, cook, maid, laundress, valet, secretary, book-keeper. To your grandparents: a child, an adult, an equal, a friend, and, in their later years, a mother. For a mother there is no such thing as an eight-hour day or a forty-hour week! And yet she will always have time to listen to and sympathize with your highs, your lows, your ups, your downs, your smiles, your frowns. Like Eliza for Professor 'Iggins in *My Fair Lady*, for your mother *you* almost make the day begin. And there isn't one daughter among us who can say that we've always brought our mothers fair weather. Nor

174

does she expect it, because, although she may seem well advanced in years to you, she really isn't too far away from being a young daughter herself.

A fortunate girl you are indeed if you have a loving mother; a great plus factor in your world of women is a sister, too. A good sister is really part of you. To your sister you can bare your innermost thoughts and know the facts will be kept inviolate. If she's older, she'll straighten you out fast—by cuffing, pushing, and biting when you're a toddler; by talking it out, advising, counseling later. She will save you—and your mother—a lot of needless wonder and worry, and give you all many extra hours a week for the fun and sharing that make for so much happiness in a family. If your sister is younger, it is up to you to lead in constructive measures. A good sister relationship is one of the greatest luxuries in all human experience.

Brothers have a special kind of value for you. An older brother can be one of the best friends you'll ever have: a pal, a young father, a magnificent teacher, a wise, inspired, and tender counselor. A younger brother—who adores you, teases you, hides your prize possessions, doesn't give you a moment's peace, heckles you to tears and then loves you so he can't be budged more than an inch away from you— is about the best training you will ever get for motherhood. You will achieve patience, laughter, indulgence, wisdom, and womanliness through your relationship with him; and, one day, he will be grown up and guiding you!

And those of you who are fortunate in having a big family will often have others in the family group who are especially dear to you —an aunt, grandparents, cousins, nieces, and nephews.

There is so much give-and-take in a good family life that it is important to think for a minute about your own special place in the family. What do you give? Love that shines through all you do every day of your life. Affection that is demonstrated by some of you with a good-morning and good-night kiss; the going to the door with your father when he leaves in the morning, the welcome home; the spontaneous hug for your mother when you are happy; the comforting kiss for your brother or sister who is hurt or unhappy. The loving kindness that inspires you to do something to help someone you love or to share a treat or a surprise or a dream with him. The cheerful carrying out of family duties, whether yours is a big one like getting supper every Sunday or a small, steady one like emptying the wastebaskets every morning. The respect and loyalty you owe each member of your family—respect for the relationships of each person; loyalty that tells you to keep family differences, problems, business, and finances a family matter that is not to be discussed with outsiders. And you also give laughter and fun; a happy home should ring with laughter much of the time, so you do your share of making it ring.

What do you take from family living? Love, affection, and companionship. Unlimited faith, unwavering support, and sympathy. The best your parents can provide in the way of food, clothing, education, and opportunities to grow. A world of fun and warmth within the secure walls of your home. . . . Guidance is yours, too, if you are willing to take it. You will not always follow in the path your parents guide you; but when you don't, show them the courtesy of agreeing with their principles, even if you can't agree with their methods. Try to understand the motivating reasons behind your parents' desire for you to benefit from what they have learned. And remember that any difference of opinion is made the less by phrases like "I'm sure you're right, but . . ." "I'll try to do exactly as you would like, but . . ." "I do agree with you, but could I . . ." or "I'm not sure, but I think. . . ." The sure thing to be wary of in any discussions is the flat accusation that starts out "You *always* . . ." "Why do you have to . . ." "*Other* girls. . . ." That sort of remark will only remind your parents of the days when you were a positive six-year-old, and you

176

will have thoroughly weakened any strong position you might have held in the discussion.

Each family—like each organization—has its discipline to maintain. In business it's called company policy, in the army and navy it's called regulations.

Discipline is a good word to understand. Discipline is a way of life, an orderly conduct of a group. Don't confuse it with punishment. You will always be subject to discipline, whether it's imposed by your family or your school or your church, or, as you grow in personality and maturity, by yourself. The basis of all discipline is to assure happiness, comfort, and peace to the group and to each member of the group. It sets the basis for self-discipline, the order we all must live by in adult life. Your responsibility as a young adult is to study and appreciate the discipline set down for your good and the good of your family. There are very few parents today—and I doubt there were many yesterday!—who require the unflinching, unquestioning acceptance of family rules demanded by the astonishing father of Elsie Dinsmore. So when you are confused by family discipline, you can probably find out the good reasons behind it—and seek an adjustment—if you wait till a time when your parents are relaxed and have the time and mood to talk.

The other adults in your world—your teachers, club leaders, camp leaders, and, to a lesser degree, those who employ you both on a part-time and a regular basis—are in a way your family, too. You've heard your father say of a much-respected and loved boss, "He's like a father to me." A favorite teacher can often be as close to you as a young aunt or an older sister. When you are away from home, you may feel that one of your mother's friends in that town is almost a mother to you—or a senior counselor or director of a camp may be a big sister or a mother to you. Girls who have known the warmth of a close-knit family group will often seek the affection of a substitute family when they are away from home—a girl who has known the companionship of sisters may marry and move far away; more likely than not, she will try to "fill in" the missing family with new friends who remind her of those she loves and is separated from.

The other adults in your world deserve the same give-and-take of respect, loyalty, and responsibility that you owe your family. To be happy, you must make others happy—the friends of your young world, the friends of the adult world that surrounds you, and, most of all, the family you love. The universe consists of billions of little worlds; and the stronger and happier you make each of *your* worlds, the greater chance there is for all mankind to rededicate the universe to the ideal in which God created it.

2. *The College Try*

AT ONE TIME or another every girl considers the possibility of going to college—the fun, the friends, the knowledge to be gained, all make the college education an all-American ideal. Certainly a good education helps a girl to get along better in the world. Those girls who have earned *a high-school degree alone* have an earning power 30 per cent higher than girls who fail to finish high school. I am not convinced that every girl needs or should go to college. Some with outstanding ability in a special field might do better to go to a specialist school—art, interior design, music, and so on. Others, who plan to marry young, might do better to get a good business training either in secretarial school or in a trade such as dressmaking or photography or hairdressing, so they can help fatten the family income while their husbands attend college.

But if you sincerely want the values of a liberal or specialized college education, it is within your reach despite all you hear about the difficulties of obtaining entrance to a college these days. Don't fret too much about your ability. If your sights are set within the limits of your capabilities, going to college is not only possible for you it is also not too difficult. But—you must be willing to work toward this goal and *plan ahead*. Not like the sign I see in so many offices that says

P L A N A H EA
D

What is the situation today? There are certainly more boys and girls who plan to go to college in the next five years than there were in the last five, so the situation is more competitive. However, there are 2,189 institutions which qualify as colleges or universities in the United States. Only a few score have substantially more applicants than they can handle, which means that, family traditions and heart-felt wishes to the contrary, every girl can't go to Smith, nor can every boy go to Princeton.

Then, too, many state colleges are required by law to accept any resident of the state who is a graduate of an accredited high school—this is fine for residents but not so good for out-of-staters.

Will a good rating on your College Boards help? It certainly won't hurt, particularly in the approximately 180 schools which require some use of College Entrance Examination Board Testing. But whether or not you go to one of the schools in the College Board group, you can glean a considerable amount of useful information from the fine handbook the group puts out. It's titled *The College Handbook*, and you can order it for one dollar from The College Entrance Examination Board, either at P.O. Box 592, Princeton, New Jersey, or P.O. Box 27896, Los Angeles 27, California.

Planning ahead   Sometime in your second or third year of high school, I think you would be very wise to make a plan of action, first deciding which four schools you would like to go to. Analyze your qualifications honestly, so that you don't aim too high or too low; and let your choice spread over four schools of varying degrees of difficulty in gaining entrance.

Once you've determined your choice, talk it over with your school's college counselor—or, if no counselor is available, a friendly teacher.

The good habits of study we worked out in the "Take the Matter of Your Mind" chapter should help you to get the best marks you possibly can; and, in this connection, you will find some comfort in knowing that good marks come easily to only one in a million—the young people you know who seem to get good marks without much effort probably have superb work habits. While many colleges will take those who put on steam only in the last year of school, a consistently good academic average is your best passport to the college of your choice.

You'll want to apply at the colleges you've chosen in your junior year of high school. Certainly no later than the beginning of your senior year.

It's unusual for teen-agers to know what type of education they want in college. If you are one of those who have determined on a field at an early age—medicine, nursing, business administration, teaching, law—your academic channels are well marked for you. If not, take a good liberal arts course and see where your interests lead you.

If your marks have been rather consistently below average but you still yearn to go to college, keep your hopes up. You can still make a good college. Give yourself time to analyze what the colleges of your choice are looking for by writing for catalogs and by studying them. If possible, after this study, visit the schools and talk with admitting officers; your interest in going to their college, your effort in making the trip, and your personality can really help.

What is the college looking for? Colleges, like people, are not all alike. Some want College Entrance Examination Board achievement and aptitude tests taken in the third or fourth year of high school. Some want fifteen, others want sixteen, high-school credits (one year in one major subject equals one credit).

All of them want to know your scholastic record and your principal's or headmistress's opinion of you, and they will get those directly from your school.

And all of them would prefer to have an interview with you, but sometimes distance makes that impossible. Most will ask you to write a history of yourself in your application, and all will ask for personal references. On this latter, restraint is in order: your minister, doctor, or family lawyer could be one; an alumna who knows you well could be another; and a close friend of your family could be a third. Incidentally, it's a pleasant courtesy for you to send a brief note to the person you've given as reference and say you have applied at Blank College and you hope she won't mind your giving her name as a reference.

Once all the facts are in, the school will analyze you in terms of rather intangible values. These are:

- Your personal integrity—that's a broad value, but it narrows down to how active you've been in church or social work, whether you've taken on any family obligations either in time or by earning money, whether you've helped with the farm, the store, the office—in other words, whether you've demonstrated a concern for the well-being of others.

- How much get-up-and-go you've demonstrated—if you've had summer jobs, worked after school, started a nursery school group after school hours, developed a small mail-order business, won a 4-H sewing contest, edited the school newspaper, acted as school representative for a clothing store, or whatever. Activities such as these display your initiative and energy.

- The inquisitiveness of your mind—whether you're hungry to learn, to do, to explore, to see new things.

- Whether you've done something besides study—not too many things, please, but music, dance, sports, business are indicative of the breadth of your interests.

These are your personal qualities through which your personality shines and these are the plus values that can help to overcome a mediocre academic record.

What are you looking for in a college?   One you can afford, certainly! In *The College Handbook* the average costs are anywhere from slightly below $1,000 a year for a boarding student to more than $2,000. Of course, scholarships help, and jobs are sometimes available, but you might as well set your heart on colleges you can afford. You will also want to decide whether to choose a coeducational college, and your parents' advice is a big help here.

Incidentally, unless your family is very well off and is not facing a lot of tuitions to pay at once, you might want to investigate the subject of scholarships or loans to help ease your financial way through college. If you hope for a scholarship, you will need to apply for both admission and a scholarship as early as possible in your senior high-school year. If you need a scholarship, you will be wise to investigate scholarship possibilities before you determine on a college—another college might offer you more aid. In addition to grants from individual schools, there are also many programs of financial aid sponsored by foundations, businesses, religious or fraternal groups.

The College Handbook, mentioned in the beginning of this chapter, has an excellent section on scholarships, as well as detailed information on grants available at the 180 schools of the College Board group. You may also want to go to your library and read more on the subject. These books will help you:

SCHOLARSHIPS, FELLOWSHIPS AND LOANS, by S. Norman Finegold. Cambridge, Massachusetts: Bellman Publishing Company.

LOVEJOY'S COLLEGE GUIDE, by Clarence E. Lovejoy. New York: Simon and Schuster, Inc.

SCHOLARSHIPS AND FELLOWSHIPS AVAILABLE AT INSTITUTIONS OF HIGHER EDUCATION, by Therese Birch Wilkins. (United States Office of Education Bulletin No. 16) Washington, D. C.: Government Printing Office.

THE COLLEGE BLUE BOOK, by Christian E. Burckel and Huber William Hurt. New York: Christian E. Burckel and Associates.

How far away from home do you want to go, remembering that travel is expensive and that one of the paradoxical joys of college is getting home to your family and friends for holidays?

Does the college offer the courses you want—nursing, premed, architecture, and so on?

What is the size and type of the college—large, small, city, country, private, state, church-connected? (Your local public library will have three or four books that describe every college in the country.)

Finally, what do you and your counselors think of your chances to get in the four colleges of your choice?

College is a marvelous experience and one I hope you'll enjoy if you truly want it. But do remember this—many of the happiest wives and mothers, many of the most successful women in business—and men, too!—never went to college; and many of those who did never finished. So if you don't make college—or if you find you can't afford to go to college—there are wide worlds still open for you to conquer.

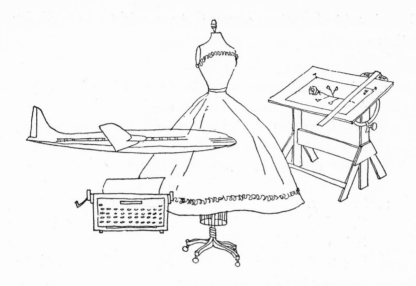

3. *Careers Without College*

THERE ARE FINE careers open to girls who have completed high school, and you can forge your way to a better job in many of these if you have the time and the money to go to a school that specializes in training for the field of your choice. (You can also, of course, go to a specialist school after you have finished all or part of college.)

The vocational advisory service at your school or your public library or Chamber of Commerce should be able to give you a list of schools in or near your community where you can get specialized training, and often they can tell you the length of time such a course would take and the cost of the tuition.

Here is a list of fourteen careers that you might find worth investigating:

1. *Air-lines hostess or reservationist.* Qualifications vary, with some air lines requiring two years of college or nurse's training. A visit or a letter to the nearest office of each air line that serves your area will bring you the details of each line's training program.

2. *Secretary.* This is an opening wedge into junior executive jobs in all fields except those that require qualified training (like law, medicine, engineering). It can also lead to the rewarding and well-paid job of executive secretary or office manager.

3. *Interior decorating.* In some cases you can get a job as an apprentice without special training; but if you are serious about the field, you will also take decorating courses at night or embark on a well-planned course of intensive reading and home study in decorating, architecture, furniture, silver, textiles, and related subjects.

4. *Nursing.* You have a choice of practical, registered, or baby nursing. Write to The National League for Nursing, 2 Park Avenue, New York, New York, for more information; and talk to your doctor and to the directors of nursing at your local hospitals. It is obvious to any female that any nursing training—including nurse's-aide courses—is of invaluable help to a wife and mother. It is often possible for those who choose to be a registered nurse to take additional courses that will lead to a Bachelor of Science degree.

5. *Fashion.* This is a broad field that includes merchandising (assistant buyer, buyer, merchandise manager of women's and children's clothing, fashion co-ordinator, working as liaison with the buyers, display departments, advertising and public-relations department, and the press; designer, or publicity of sales representative for a manufacturer). Many stores have special training squads, often requiring some college; and there are many colleges with special courses in fashion, and some schools whose sole or main interest is fashion.

6. *Art.* Here the opportunities range from advertising and magazine layout, to fashion sketching, illustration, package designing, industrial design, interior design, architecture, architectural or mechanical drafting, and many others.

7. *Technicians and aides for laboratories* of all kinds are in demand—medical, pharmaceutical, technological, and so on. The fields open to you will depend largely on the kinds of industries in your vicinity.

8. *Dietitian's aide and public-health nutritionist.* The hospitals and visiting service in your town can advise you on these fields.

9. *Beauty.* Both as an industry and as a small enterprise, beauty culture and hairdressing are big business. Sometimes you can get apprentice training in a shop, but you will eventually have to pass an examination and get a license to practice.

10. *Travel agent or reservationist.*

11. *Dental hygienist.*

12. *Real estate broker.*

13. *Public accountant.* You'll need two years' training for this.

14. *Photography.* Here you can often start as a girl Friday, work up to darkroom technician, and eventually learn photography.

The variety of your opportunities will depend really on three things—first, the amount of investigating you do to discover the training programs that are open to you; second, the number of training programs available to you in your community; third, your willingness and financial ability to go to the nearest city where you can get the training you want in the field you choose.

The investigating, the training, the possible travel, and the career itself will all open more and more doors that will lead you to new friends, new interests, and the unfolding of your bright, maturing personality.

4. Choosing a Job

NOW THAT YOU have almost completed the path of growth that has brought you from childhood through your adolescent years, the question of choosing a job becomes paramount to you. Whether it's a summer job or a permanent one, you are entering the adult world of business and your approach needs to be very business-like indeed.

I think most girls realize that choosing a permanent job is a serious undertaking because today many women—including those with children—work all or a good part of their married lives. But I feel that a serious approach to a summer job is often lacking. These few summers you have to explore the business world can be of invaluable help to you when you apply for college or specialist school admission, when you are in college, when you choose your college major or determine on a business career, when you are married (whether or not you work after marrying). A summer job is, in a way, a synthesis of a course at a business college.

How do you go about getting a summer job? First, you need to survey the kinds that might be available. Ask your friends what they plan to do. Ask your parents, other adults if they know of any summer jobs that you might be eligible for. Try your school's employment counselor. And read the newspaper advertisements, but discuss them with your family before answering or going for an interview.

Those are the jobs that are available. Then there is a second, often better group of jobs that calls on your energy, enterprise, and initiative—and is frequently worth the extra effort, both in experience and money earned. That is to think what kind of service your neighbors might be willing to buy. "Service" could include organizing a day camp for young children, sports instruction for older ones, handmade sock knitting, a morning play school, homemade desserts, catering for barbecues, shopping, mending, or silver polishing. Whatever service is most needed in your neighborhood will be the one for which you might get the largest number of customers. The ideal would be to have enough business so you could afford one or two other girls to help you. And you will want to organize your working schedule so that you have enough time for eight hours' sleep, meals on time, fun with your family and friends, and reading time for your summer book report. Good working habits are as important as good study habits; there is always an emergency when you do have to study or work overtime, but if overtime becomes usual rather than unusual, you need to analyze your plan of work.

Whatever kind of job you do in the summer, you will probably gain much more from it than the money you are paid; so, if you have a choice of several jobs, do choose the one that will give you the biggest return not so much in terms of money as in terms of background and experience.

How do you go about getting a permanent job?   My first recommendation would be to talk to people who are successful in many different fields, and your family and friends can give you a great deal of help here. When you talk to them, take a list of questions with you that reads something like this:

- What kinds of jobs might be open to me in your field?
- What would be the best job I might hope for if I succeeded in your field?
- What would be the approximate time it would take me—if I worked really seriously—to achieve a job like that?
- Would I need to supplement my present education with any special studies or skills?
- What might I hope for in terms of salary if I should be successful in your field?
- Would you tell me the names of a few companies in your field where I might apply for a beginning job?

Then, perhaps after some discussion with your family and close friends—or perhaps by yourself—you will decide on the field that most interests you and for which you think you are qualified. In addition to talking to people in various fields, you may want to read more about them, so at the end of this chapter you will find a list of books that I think you might enjoy.

Once the field is set, a helpful thing to do would be to list the companies in that field and, beside the name of each company, to put the names of the people you know in the company—or the people whom your family or friends could introduce you to.

Your next step would be to ask for an appointment with each person. When they see you, your approach is very simple. You say, "I would like very much to work in the whatever-it-is business. And I would be very grateful to you if you would tell me what would be the best way to get started in it." Better be prepared for a wide variety of answers, ranging from, "It would be easier if you had several years of business-school training in back of you . . ." to, "Well, we never hire beginners in this company . . ." to, "Don't you think it would be better if you tried a less exacting field? . . ." to the dream answer that comes true every so often, "Let me call the personnel director. He was telling me only yesterday that we're in the market for some bright young people."

Despite all the stiff-upper-lip and/or Horace Greeley comments to the contrary, it is not necessarily the brightest move to attempt to get a job on your own without any kind of assist from your family or friends. I'm not sure I don't think it's a touch of the archaic. One example of how to put your family and friends to practical job-hunting use is this: A young friend of mine had set her heart on getting a beginning job in advertising and, although she was energetically pursuing every lead she was given or could manufacture, she wasn't too proud to accept her mother's hesitant suggestion that she might ask the advice of an executive of an advertising agency. She called, said, "Allen, Anne wants very much to work in advertising. Is there any advice you might give me that would help her to get into your field?" Allen's answer was, "Well, I think I would do exactly what you're doing now—call a friend in the agency business! As a matter of fact, we're looking for a number of people and Anne just might fill one of the places."

Anne—who did get the job—didn't have it handed to her on a silver platter; she had to sell herself to the personnel director and the head of the department where she eventually went to work. She had to take a number of aptitude and personality tests, all of which she did well in. But it helped to know where to expend her efforts in seeking a job.

Once you have been employed in the field of your choice for a few months, you should set up some goals for your own job future in the field. After you get your first promotion or raise—in other words, when you've proven yourself a little—discuss these goals with your boss or some executive of the firm other than the personnel director. Your boss can guide you in choosing after-hours subjects to take—mechanical drawing, certain science courses, fashion sketching, or whatever is applicable to your field; he can review your goals to be sure you are heading in the direction where your talents are. And he will remember your serious ambition, especially when better jobs open up in your company.

If after a year or two you come to the rueful conclusion that you haven't made any one of your goals and are getting nowhere fast, you will want to consider shifting to another field. Time has a way of slipping by, so if you don't give yourself some time limits, you may get beyond the age when other companies would consider you as a trainee and a potentially valuable employee.

If you are undecided about what field to enter

It is always probable that, when you first start working, you may not be able to decide on a specific field. In that case, my advice would be to seek the kind of general business background that would make you a more valuable employee in the field you eventually choose. One of the best concentrated sources of business training is the selling field, and if you are still groping for your eventual career, try for a job in a department store or in the largest, busiest dress shop in your town. Most businesses are concerned with making or buying a product and then marketing it at the best possible price, and this is one of the processes you learn firsthand when you sell. You can also become a specialist in a field such as fashion, beauty, home furnishings, or children's clothing and go on from there to a job with a manufacturer, a newspaper's woman's page, a radio or TV station, a magazine, an advertising or public-relations agency.

Business etiquette

There are certain rules of business etiquette that you will need to add to your already good manners. Here are some of them:

- Always write a brief letter to thank anyone who has been kind enough to interview you, whether or not you like the field or the company or the job involved. This is not only good manners but good sense, because Mr. Whitaker of the Blank Company might move on to the Grand Company where you would very much like to work.

- The first few months you are in a new job, learn rather than lead or teach. No matter how good your ideas are, they won't meet with much success if the rest of the company looks on you as the girl wonder (translated: general threat to everyone's job).

- Observe company office hours without being conspicuous. In other words, if the office opens at nine and everyone else arrives by tacit agreement at nine-fifteen, you will gain nothing by arriving virtuously at eight-forty-five or self-confidently at nine-thirty. The same goes for closing hour.

- You can be shining, hard-working, neat, and pretty as a picture—but, more important, be good-natured about whatever you are asked to do.

- Office gossip may be universal and occasionally you may glean some gem of useful information. On the whole, it hurts both gossiper and those who listen.

- Clothes, hairdo, make-up, and perfume should all be conservative, and probably your best tip here is to study the successful, well-dressed young women executives in your company and to style your own office appearance in the same spirit.

- Many companies spend large sums of money to make their offices as soundproof and noiseless as possible. Jangly bracelets, clattering shoes, much banging of doors, drawers, and books, and chatter and laughing can make the whole effort seem wasted. The noisemaker will not endear herself to the management.

- Good common sense is a fine business asset. It tells you not to dart at your superior with one question at a time, but to wait till you have three or four to discuss. It tells you to co-operate with the spirit of the company's rules. It tells you to go slow in making office friendships, never to call a superior by his or her first name until you have been invited to. It tells you to keep company business private to the company—unless it is information that has been released to the newspapers.

Working at a job you like is part of your wonderful American heritage. You have the freedom of choice to work where you want to and at what you want. Business and government team their efforts to give you every safeguard and security during your working years and in the faraway days of your retirement. The free enterprise that has made American business so great a force in keeping our country strong and free brings you many blessings and bounties; it also brings you the responsibility of doing your job the very best you know how. You and every person who works *are* American Business.

You will find a lot of direction signals about the career for *you* in some of the excellent books available today. Here is a list of books you might look into, which will help to guide you in choosing what you would most like to do.

General

CAREER PLANNING FOR HIGH SCHOOL STUDENTS, by William J. Reilly. New York: Harper and Brothers, 1953.

CUES FOR CAREERS, by Judith Scott and Macrae Unger. Philadelphia: Macrae Smith Company, 1954.

From High School to a Job, by Adrian R. Paradis. New York: David McKay Company, Inc., 1954.

How to Find the Right Vocation, by Harry D. Kitson. New York: Harper and Brothers, 1947.

How to Get and Hold the Job You Want, by Ruth Hooper Larison. New York: Longmans, Green and Company, Inc., 1950.

I Find My Vocation, 4th edition, by Harry Dexter Kitson. New York: McGraw-Hill Book Company, 1954.

Occupational Outlook Handbook, by Bureau of Labor Statistics. Washington 25, D.C.: United States Government Printing Office.

Planning Your Future, 4th edition, by George E. Myers, Gladys M. Little, Sarah A. Robinson. New York: McGraw-Hill Book Company, 1954.

Vocations for Girls, revised edition, by Mary Rebecca Lingenfelter and Harry Dexter Kitson. New York: Harcourt, Brace and Company, 1951.

Womanpower, by National Manpower Council. New York: Columbia University Press, 1957.

Special Fields

Advertising as a Career, by Mark O'Dea. Pleasantville, New York: Printer's Ink Publishing Company, Inc., 1945.

Assignment in Modeling, by Helen Fraser. New York: McGraw-Hill Book Company, 1950.

Career Bulletins, by American Home Economics Association. Washington, D.C.

Career Opportunities in Home Economics in Business, by Home Economics in Business Department of the American Home Economics Association. Washington, D.C.: 1954.

Career for Nurses, 2nd edition, by Dorothy Deming. New York: McGraw-Hill Book Company, 1952.

Careers for Specialized Secretaries, by Juvenal Angel. New York: World Trade Academy Press, Inc., 1952.

Career in Cartooning, by Lawrence Lariar. New York: Dodd, Mead and Company, 1950.

CAREERS IN COMMERCIAL ART, new revised edition, by J. I. Biegeleisen. New York: E. P. Dutton and Company, Inc., 1952.

CAREERS IN PHOTOGRAPHY, by C. B. Neblette. Rochester, New York: Rochester Institute of Technology, 1953.

CAREERS IN THE ARTS: FINE AND APPLIED, by Elizabeth McCausland. New York: The John Day Company, 1950.

CAREERS IN THE WORLD OF FASHION, by Frieda Curtis. New York: Whiteside, Inc., 1953.

THE DEPARTMENT STORE STORY, by Frank M. Mayfield. New York: Fairchild Publications, Inc., 1949.

HEALTH CAREERS GUIDEBOOK, by Zelpha C. Franklin. Washington, D.C.: The National Health Council, 1955.

HOW TO BE A SUCCESSFUL ADVERTISING WOMAN, edited by Mary McBride. New York: Whittlesey House, McGraw-Hill Book Company, 1948.

JOBS THAT TAKE YOU PLACES, revised edition, by Joseph Leeming. New York: David McKay Company, Inc., 1953.

KEYS TO A FASHION CAREER, by The Fashion Group, Inc. New York: McGraw-Hill Book Company, 1946.

A NEW HORIZON IN RECREATION, by Charles Vettiner. New York: Horizon Press, Inc., 1956.

OPPORTUNITIES IN BEAUTY CULTURE, by Florence E. Wall. New York: Vocational Guidance Manuals, Inc., 1952.

OPPORTUNITIES IN CERAMICS, by Samuel Ray Scholes. New York: Vocational Guidance Manuals, Inc., 1953.

OPPORTUNITIES IN FASHION, by Alida Vreeland. New York: Vocational Guidance Manuals, Inc., 1951.

OPPORTUNITIES IN LIBRARY CAREERS, by Robert E. Kingery. New York: Vocational Guidance Manuals, Inc., 1952.

SKYGIRL, by Mary F. Murray. New York: Duell, Sloan and Pearce, Inc., 1951.

THE STORY OF NURSING, by Bertha S. Dodge. Boston: Little, Brown and Company, 1954.

YOUR PLACE IN TV: A HANDY GUIDE FOR YOUNG PEOPLE, by Edwin B. Broderick. New York: David McKay Company, Inc., 1954.

5. *You'll Make a Lovely Bride*

ALL BRIDES ARE lovely, and the most wonderful wedding present any fairy godmother could give a bride would be the assurance that her husband would think her still as lovely ten, twenty, thirty years after her wedding day. "They lived happily ever after" is the classic ending to a love story—five little words that describe the years of preparation, devotion, sharing, companionship, and care that go into making a successful and happy marriage.

Marriage is the greatest career a woman can have, and yet many girls—who are ready to get married but are not ready for marriage—enter matrimony with little preparation, and few goals or plans other than to live happily ever after. Like a good cake, good movie, beautiful building, or perfect jewel, a good marriage doesn't just happen. Marriages are made in heaven, they say—certainly they have to be made *happy* on earth!

198

What does make a good marriage? If you and your husband have a community of interests—the same kind of family background, education, religion, standards, and goals in life—your chances for happiness are much greater than if you differ widely on these important pillars of your life. A great romance with someone fascinating and different makes very good reading, but a warmly responsive affection for and from the boy next door makes a much better marriage. (Incidentally, "the boy next door" in this case can often mean a boy from the next town or the next state—or one seven states away—whose family and upbringing are like your family and your upbringing.)

When you marry you are not merely having a sanctioned love affair. You and your husband are starting to build a family life. Even if you should never be blessed with children (your own or adopted) you two will be a family unit in your community; and though you may not yet appreciate it, the contentment, stability, and worth of your particular family unit—whether it's a small or a large family—affect the well-being of your community and your country. You are partners with a lifetime interest in a growing concern.

What will you need to contribute to this partnership to make it a successful one? First of all—love, tenderness, and affection. A great deal is written on the subject of love in marriage both from the spiritual and the physical viewpoints. It seems to me that any girl who is engaged to be married would do well to arrange at least one visit with her clergyman to discuss the spiritual side of wedded love, and to arrange a visit with her mother's doctor or the family doctor to discuss the physical responsibilities and rewards of love. Both your clergyman and your doctor are specialists in human relationships and frequently are called upon to act as marriage counselors, so they are well qualified to help guide you—and your fiancé, too.

You will also contribute the thought, consideration, skill, and efficiency that go into the making of a pleasant home carefully run within the family's means. The responsibility for planning and serving attractive, healthful meals is yours, too. Your mother can guide you here and perhaps you have had homemaking courses at your school; but probably your best teacher will be your husband, since you will want to run the house and prepare the meals the way he wants them. However, you should know the basic skills of making coffee, cooking eggs, broiling and roasting meats, and preparing vegetables and fruits; basic house cleaning, and how to use and care for any appliances you will have; mending, laundry, and simple repairs.

You will also have the major responsibility for the care of the children, so you would be wise, long before you are engaged, to seek the opportunities to take care of infants and little children—whether it's paid or unpaid baby-sitting—so that you will be experienced at bathing infants, feeding them, making a formula, persuading toddlers to go to bed, and so on.

You will need to show an appreciation of your husband's job and the family finances; and, most important, you will need to make a continuing contribution of emotional, spiritual, and intellectual companionship.

And you will need to satisfy his need for friends and a sense of belonging to a community.

What do you do to help your husband contribute to your marriage? Again, the first requirement is love, and his love for you will flourish only if you create the kind of happy, pleasant home where love can live. The companionship he should provide will be greater if you are skillful and talented at making emotional, spiritual, and intellectual companionship with you attractive and necessary to him. But much of the fun and sharing of little "anniversary" dinners, the excursions for old times' sake, the tickets for the play, seeing the new exhibit at the museum, making the new and interesting books available to him, will be the result of your planning.

Husbands, by tradition, contribute the major part of the family's income; your pleasure here is to inspire him in his work, to be interested in the day-to-day challenge of his business, to encourage him in his dreams for the future. In this connection, I'm sure you have heard the remark, "Back of every successful man there is a woman."

And there is one especially great contribution your husband can make to your marriage if you will give him your wholehearted help. This is leadership. We all say marriage is a partnership and, for the most part, we mean it in the sense of sharing the fun, the joys, the responsibilities, the highs and lows of any family's life. But just as there can be only one skipper to a boat, one driver to a car, or one president of a company, so there can be only one head of a happy house—and that is, by law, by taxes, by census, and by woman's intuition, the husband.

It's a pleasant thought to remember that if a man's home is his castle, he must be the lord and master; and you, therefore, are the chatelaine, the mistress of the castle and keeper of the keys to a very happy existence as a wedded wife.

The Keys of C

MORE often than not, we think of a key as a means of opening a door—to something we want, to something new, perhaps to a whole new world. And, indeed, in this book we have looked for the keys that will make your world of young living the best of all possible worlds.

But now, for a moment, I would like to think of keys in another sense. Whether or not the art of creating music is one of your special talents, you have gleaned a basic musical knowledge in school and at home—and the key of C is one you know and recognize. A key in music means the total harmonic and melodic relations of a family of tones, and the key of C is called *natural* because the scale is played on the "naturals," or white keys of a keyboard.

Living with people—in your family and in the world—also calls for total harmonic and melodic relations in a natural key. So, in order that your spontaneous everyday behavior will create this harmony and melody of life, here are ten C words that are your keys to richly rewarding happiness for you and those you know and love:

202

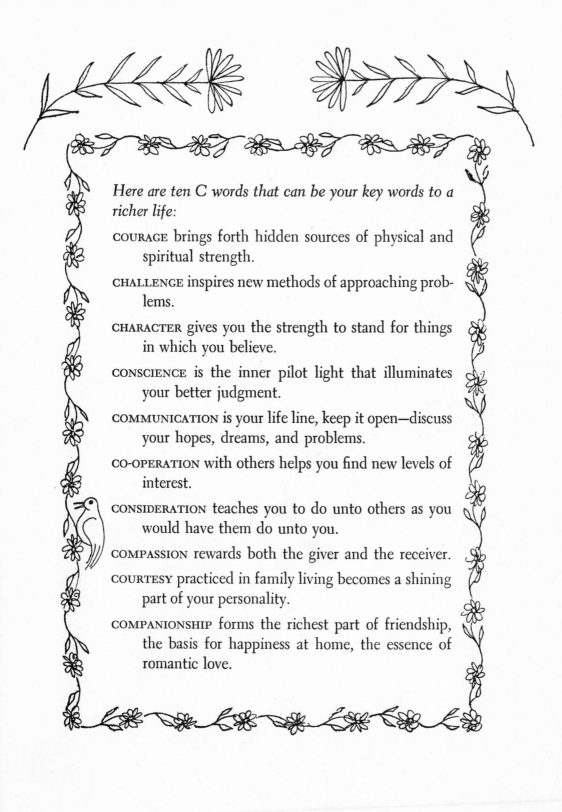

Here are ten C words that can be your key words to a richer life:

COURAGE brings forth hidden sources of physical and spiritual strength.

CHALLENGE inspires new methods of approaching problems.

CHARACTER gives you the strength to stand for things in which you believe.

CONSCIENCE is the inner pilot light that illuminates your better judgment.

COMMUNICATION is your life line, keep it open—discuss your hopes, dreams, and problems.

CO-OPERATION with others helps you find new levels of interest.

CONSIDERATION teaches you to do unto others as you would have them do unto you.

COMPASSION rewards both the giver and the receiver.

COURTESY practiced in family living becomes a shining part of your personality.

COMPANIONSHIP forms the richest part of friendship, the basis for happiness at home, the essence of romantic love.

THE
seventeen
PARTY NOTEBOOK

Introduction

There used to be an advertising slogan that read, "The man with the plans gets there!" and while your goal is not to be the hostess with the mostes'—making party giving your career—you do need to have a plan any time you entertain. Whether it's an elaborate schedule for a big party or a simple one for a small party, you will get there as a successful hostess if you have a plan.

So this section is the beginning of your party notebook, to help you and your guests have a wonderful time.

ICEBREAKERS

Sometimes it's hard to get a party started; perhaps all the guests don't know each other, perhaps you're all just starting to go to grown-up parties. In any case, something has to be done and you, the hostess, are the one to do it. Here are some ideas that might help you to change that hostess's horror, the tableau—where everyone stands posed and silent—into a lively, merry party:

flower teams fill a tray with clusters of flowers for the girls and another with matching boutonnieres for the boys. Put one tray in your room and, as each girl leaves her wrap, give her a flower to wear. Meantime have the boy who is acting as host hand out the boutonnieres. Then each boy finds the matching girl and talks to her or dances with her. Makes it easy to divide the group into two teams if you play games later.

mad hatters   supply everyone with a hat shape and put a big basket of trimmings in the middle of the table; then get everyone to work and award small prizes for the prettiest, worst, maddest hats that are produced. You can collect a lot of old hats and strip off the trimmings—or buy some inexpensive hat shapes at the dime store—or get paper hats. Trimmings could include everything you and your friends could collect from old hats, your mother's trimming box (ask her first!); real flowers and leaves, ribbons and paper ribbons; newspapers, crepe paper, construction paper; toys, and so on. This is a wonderful device to get a group of people to feel silly, relaxed, and like having fun.

brightly colored balloons   these make a festive party, especially when used in games with prizes to be won. You have the balloons strung up on the ceiling (after inserting one or two prizes —handkerchiefs for girls, ties for boys, or just a piece of paper notifying the winner—in the balloons before they are blown up), then toward the end of the party cut the string and the guests will use their own methods of bursting the balloons. The balloon dance, however, takes quite a bit of space and should not be attempted in small rooms or where too many breakable things might be imperiled!

Another version of the balloon dance is to give each couple a balloon to balance between their foreheads; the couple who dance the longest without dropping or breaking the balloon win a prize.

208

musical chairs   the perennial party game is always fun for starting a dancing party. So is the *circle dance*, where the boys make a circle around the girls, who are also in a circle. When the music starts, the girls' circle moves one way and the boys' the other. When the music stops, the boy in front of the girl is her next partner.

string portraits   write down the names of each guest on a separate slip of paper. When you have everyone seated, explain that each guest is to make a string portrait of the face of the boy or girl whose name will be on the slip he will receive—and that he is to keep the name a secret. Each person gets a sheet of construction paper and a saucer of paste. In the middle of the table—or tables—put a box containing pieces of bright-colored knitting wool cut in strips about eight inches long. Each strip is dipped in the paste then put on construction paper to form eyes, mouth, hair, eyelashes, earrings, or tie, and so on. You might let everyone guess who is the subject of each portrait, keep a tally of the count, and give a small prize to the winner. And each guest should take his or her own portrait home.

puzzle starters   having a jigsaw puzzle contest is another good icebreaker. Let guests draw numbers, then go to tables marked with their numbers. When you blow the whistle, the teams start to put the puzzles together.

crazy band   collect all the toy instruments you can, plus a washboard and five thimbles, empty soda bottles and full soda bottles and sticks to tap them, sets of two dowels or sticks to tap together, sets of two blocks covered with sandpaper, a horseshoe or triangle and a spoon to ring it with, bells, an empty cigar box with rubber bands for strings, a tissue-covered comb, and so on. Then get a few good singers to start humming marches ("Yellow

209

Rose of Texas," "When the Saints Go Marching In," "Hail to the Chief," etc. . . .).

psych. study this is good for lots of laughs because even those who really can't draw a straight line with a ruler can make astonishingly charming or funny likenesses. The method is simple: Each guest sits at a table or on the floor, is given a sheet of paper and a crayon or soft pencil, and draws a picture of his or her date—*but with his eyes tightly closed.*

game for modern artists give each couple the names of another couple—on a folded slip of paper. Have an assortment of colored paper, yarns, sequins, buttons, ribbons, cord, paper doilies, foil, tinsel, pipe cleaners, dried leaves and flowers, and toothpicks. Give each couple a shirt board, or pieces of cardboard, and a saucer of paste. The object of the game is for each couple to represent the likeness and interests of another couple. You could have ten-cent prizes for the best interpretation—the silliest, the most beautiful, the most fanciful.

SPECIAL PARTIES

Sometimes you want to have a party with a purpose; and when you plan one of these, you need to have your beau help with all the plans—just as your husband will help with your parties when you are married. You may even want to ask another couple to help if your plans turn out to be fairly involved. Your goal is to have a wonderful party, remember, not to prove you can do it yourself.

Here are some parties to consider:

world travelers you need to have everyone on your dinner committee for this one! Each girl serves one course of the dinner

210

at her house. Each house represents a different country, if you mix your menus; or is decorated in the national theme of the evening, if you are using only one cuisine, to represent the country and the kind of food and party trimmings you would have if you stopped there on a round-the-world tour. Here are three kinds of travel dinners you could plan; you can either follow the scheme of using food typical of each cuisine, or you can mix them so you "stop at a different country" at each hostess's house. Choose as many courses as you want hostesses.

ORIENTAL

Stop one	China	Egg Roll (you can buy it frozen and warm it up)
Stop two	China or India	Chicken Soup with chopped spinach leaves / Curried Celery Soup (simply add curry flavor to canned soup)
Stop three	India or China	Curry of Lamb or Chicken, Green Salad / Chow Mein or Chop Suey
Stop four	China	Tea spiced with cinnamon sticks
Stop five	China	Almond Cookies (tuck a fortune under each)

CONTINENTAL

Stop one	Scandinavia	Sardines on crisp crackers and Hot Mock Glug (cinnamon sticks and raisins in hot sweet cider)
Stop two	Scotland	Scotch Broth (chicken and barley or rice soup with small white onions added)

Stop three	Germany	Frankfurters and Sauerkraut
Stop four	England	Fruit Tarts
Stop five	France	Café au Lait or Hot Chocolate
Stop six	Holland	Cheese and Crackers

LATIN

Stop one	Italy	Minestrone or Vegetable Soup with elbow noodles added to it
Stop two	Italy	Hot Green Spinach Noodles with spaghetti sauce, buttered Italian bread or Spaghetti, buttered Italian bread or Ravioli, buttered Italian bread
	or Mexico	Chili con Carne, buttered corn bread or Hot Tamales (canned) and buttered corn bread
Stop three	South America	Latin Fruit Salad (mixed avocado pears, bananas, pineapple, with garlic-flavored French dressing and scattering of small white pearl onions)
Stop four	Central America	Broiled Bananas (broiled with dusting brown sugar and butter) or Pineapple Fingers dusted with coconut
Stop five	Brazil	Mocha Cooler (coffee, instant cocoa, and sparkling water mixed and served over ice in tall glasses)

212

Decorations at each house could be little flags from each country or travel posters—or some souvenir of the country your parents or someone in your family might have, like a teapot or a coffee-pot, a piece of silver, shawl, tureen, metal or china animals, and so on. Or you could have the flowers of the country on your table—bluebells, heather, or thistles for Scotland; roses for Eng-land—or daffodils; lilies for France; etc. You might also put some songs of the country on your record player.

treasure hunts   these are fun, summer and winter. You'll be wise to consult with your parents about how far afield you need to set your treasure-hunting goals. They might take a dim view of your having matches from the golf club (eight miles away) as one clue unless the clue specifies that the match case must come from someone's house.

costume or headdress parties   these are always hilarious, especially if you have a theme—come as your favorite character in history, either with headdress or some insignia that distinguished the per-sonality. This could also be a team party—a boy and girl are invited together, and asked to represent a famous team in his-tory or literature or the arts or the entertainment world (show business offers a great variety of couples for your guests to choose from, ranging from comedians to romantic husband-wife teams). Or invite guests to come-as-you-were-when-you-were-a-baby; or come to represent a season of the year, winter, spring, summer, autumn.

new record party   everyone brings his newest record (not neces-sarily a new recording) and you all listen to it, probably get into some fine discussions.

favorite games   easy. Just pick the four favorite games in your group, play each one till the timer goes off.

names in the news   save each day's paper for two weeks before you send out invitations. Clip a name in the news (no photographs) and invite each guest to come dressed and made up to look like the name in the news.

captain's dinner   the most festive night aboard ship is the captain's dinner, and this would be a good theme for a very elegant dinner party (elegant with short cuts, of course). Ask your mother's help in setting your table to look its most handsome; besides the silver, crystal, china, and candles, you'll want to have party hats, small dishes (or ruffled paper baskets) filled with nuts, small dishes of plain and chocolate-covered mints, place cards; balloons to decorate the room; flowers. If you can clear a space for dancing during the meal—either in the dining room or in the next room—that would enhance the make-believe. Souvenir menus at each place with the ship's colors on a ribbon decoration (example: red, white, and blue for the U. S. A.; or the tricolor for France), which the girls might wear around their hair or the boys in their lapels, lend a gay and authentic touch to the table.

You'll want to simulate a formal dinner party, probably without attempting to serve each guest. My suggestion would be to have all the courses set up like a buffet—either in the dining room or, if you want to make space for dancing, in the kitchen, which you have left spick and span after your cooking. Then your guests can serve themselves and sit down at your festively decorated table.

hobo hobnob   this is a gay year-round party that's *particularly* good for summer when you can cook outdoors. Invite everyone to come dressed as a hobo. If the party's indoors, have empty tin cans or glass jars filled with weeds or flowers cut from news-

214

papers for decoration; shells or metal-foil dishes (saved from frozen meat pies) to hold vegetable sticks, candy. Supper might be a big skillet of baked beans, bread and butter, milk or coffee, packaged cookies or paper cups of ice cream with wooden spoons. In any case, guests should sit on the floor in a circle around an imaginary campfire (you could use real or Presto logs with flames cut out of red construction paper) or around the fireplace. One game to play might be to see who can write down the longest list of song titles that tie in with the theme of the party: "I've Got Plenty of Nuttin," "Hallejuh, I'm a Bum," "I Ain't Got Nobody," "There's No Place Like Home," "Nobody Knows the Trouble I've Seen," "Freight Train," and so on. Another paper game would be to list what you could buy for five cents. Still another, to list the names of railroads a hobo could hitch a ride on.

Whether you're entertaining two or twenty, boys and girls, all girls, or a mixed group of assorted ages, the method for your plans is essentially the same.

1. You work out your plans on paper: the number of guests, where you will seat them, what kind of food you will serve, what dishes you will use, when you will cook the food, how you will serve it, when and how you will clean up, and what you will need to buy for both the cooking and the cleanup.

2. You shop a day ahead of the party. With you to the store go both your shopping list and your menu. And you take advantage of all the prepared, frozen, and precooked foods that will save you time and energy.

3. You prepare as much of the food as you can the day before the party.

4. When you serve, you present the food neatly and appetizingly.
You prepare a few flower or vegetable garnishes for decorating
platters.
You mound salads high to give a more luscious look.
You make sandwiches neat with evenly sliced or rolled bread.
You serve hot foods hot—the opposite for icebox recipes.

5. You follow the secret role of all good hostesses: you have your
plans so organized that you enjoy the party as much as the guests.

Organizing your plans includes:

• making sure you have a place for men's coats and hats—this often
means clearing space in the hall closet. (Girls usually leave theirs
on your bed.)

• putting plenty of fresh soap and hand towels in bathrooms that
will be used.

• making provision—TV, bribes, or a baby-sitter if necessary—to
keep young brothers and sisters from sampling the food, trying
on guests' hats, joining the party, and other irresistible junior
tricks.

• asking a friend or two to help you with such details as
—showing guests where to put their things
—carrying food to and from the kitchen
—helping you serve
—nudging talkative guests toward the table
—nudging talkative guests away from the table
—spelling you if you're playing games, so there will be continuing activity instead of disintegration if you have to get more
punch or answer the doorbell
—spearheading the move to leave if you all have a curfew hour
or if you're going on to a movie, a game, a dance.

216

HOW TO BE A HOSTESS

There's a great deal more to having a successful party than just giving it. Since your goal is to have a smoothly pleasant party for people, it may help you to be prepared for some of the situations that will call for skillful handling by you, the hostess:

- *Sometimes one or two people are late—what do you do about serving dinner?* If they've called to let you know they'll be late—and if the delay of half an hour or less won't ruin your dinner—you explain the delay to the other guests and wait. If they've called but your dinner is not the kind that will wait willingly, you thank them for calling and say that you hope they'll forgive you if you don't wait to serve dinner—but that you'll be sure to feed them when they arrive. If they don't call, serve dinner at the time you planned; when the latecomers do arrive, say you're sorry not to have waited for them but that your dinner refused to wait. Feed them, of course.

- *Sometimes, sometimes at the last minute too, one of your guests will call and say he or she has an unexpected house guest or two.* You are pretty much obliged to extend the invitation to the house guests—even if it means setting up the bridge table and putting four people at it; actually, if I could, I would in a case like this set up several bridge tables because these would look planned, but if not, the hostess should always in this case sit at the small table.

- *Sometimes your party will freeze into groups—it's up to you to thaw them out, but how?* You can join two people and, at a lull in the conversation, suggest that you all go and ask someone in another group a question (ask an honor student if he thought the math exam was unusually difficult; ask a sports expert who will win tomorrow's game; ask a music fan about some new record-

217

ings; or ask about some local event). Or you can propel a few people to look at a painting, a plant, a picture in a new magazine, to put on a new set of records, to start the group dancing. Use the "icebreakers" (see page 207) to get a party started, and again if it stalls during the evening! The icebreakers will also help you to shuffle your guests so the groups shift and re-form—and everyone gets to talk to everyone else. This shifting of groups is also the guests' responsibility and often it just happens without planning; but you'll want to make sure it happens.

- *Sometimes you can't drag people into dinner.* This seems unreasonable but it does happen. I think your best bet here is to have a few people you can rely on firmly steer at least one other person in to the table. That will thin out the group, the stragglers will realize that they are becoming both lonely and hungry and they will come bouncing along.

- *Sometimes no one will leave the dinner table.* This is really a compliment to you and means everyone is happy and has enjoyed your cooking. If, as the Edwardians used to say, you can catch the eyes of a few guests and gather them up, you then rise and head for the living room. Serving the hot chocolate or coffee in the living room offers you the opportunity of saying, "Shall we go in the living room for coffee?"

- *Sometimes people just won't go home.* Every party has to end and a hostess has her special obligations for seeing that the festivities end in good season. The major one is that her parents have probably set a curfew hour—and so have the parents of the guests. Arrange with a close friend to get her coat and come into the group and begin saying good night. Usually, the other guests will follow her lead. Equally important—at the time, certainly!—is the obligation to have the house, the kitchen, the dishes, the pots and pans shining clean before you go to bed, so that your party does not inconvenience the rest of the family. This also lets you sleep with a clear conscience the next morning.

- *Sometimes people break things.* Even if it should be a hard break to take (one of your mother's wedding presents or a trophy of your brother's) you are honor-bound as a hostess to make your guest feel it was not a crisis; to remove the debris quickly, quietly, and neatly; to refuse nicely any offers to replace or explain; and not to mention the accident.

- *Sometimes the best of friends must part—and it's awkward if the quarrel takes place at your party.* Your best bet is quickly to think of a splendid reason for luring everyone away from the quarrelers. Your second best bet is to get the boy with the biggest heart and the most commanding persuasive personality to put an arm around each bickerer and say something along the lines of, "How about taking this rhubarb into the hall? No point in spoiling the party for everyone," or "Why don't we go out on the porch until you two cool off a bit?" or "Come on, men. Let's not make this a public fight," or "Look—you're wrecking Madge's party. Let's clear out for a few minutes."

- *Sometimes you're called to the telephone when you're having a party.* You can always handle a brief call, but if it's someone bent on a long, sociable chat, you owe it to your guests to say, "I'm awfully sorry, Liz, but I can only talk a minute—we have people here. May I call you tomorrow morning?" Then be sure you make a note to call her. Many young people are especially sensitive about not being asked to every party that's given. While this may seem foolish to you—since, obviously, everyone can't be invited at the same time—you'll want to be careful about not causing your sensitive friends to be hurt. While you can't very well deny you're having a party, you don't need to be specific about it. You can give the fact that you have guests as an excuse but you don't need to go into details about whether it's you or your family who's entertaining.

TABLE SETTINGS

Here are six diagrams to show you how to set your table properly for a luncheon, a brunch, a dinner party, a tea, a snack party, a buffet supper:

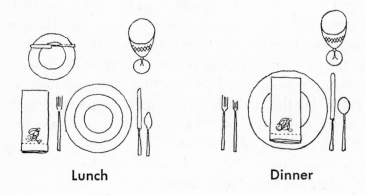

Lunch   Dinner

Brunch

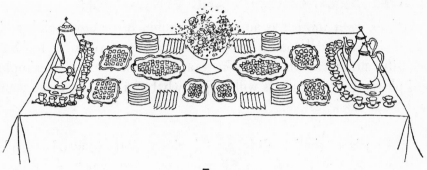

Tea

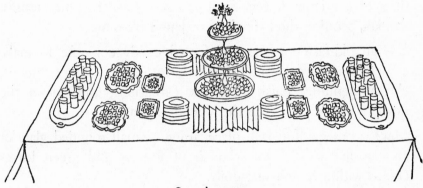

Snack party

Buffet supper

221

FLOWER ARRANGEMENTS AND CENTERPIECES

Perhaps your mother is an ardent member of a garden club and you already are well versed in the many tricks and rules for making beautiful arrangements. If you're not, some of these very simple and pleasant arrangements will be just what you need to make your party table look festive:

- Take a large shallow dish (crystal, china, pottery, wood—round, square, oblong, free-form), fill it part way with water, and float a few clusters of rhododendron or laurel leaves and the heads of three or five large flowers, such as tiger lilies, chrysanthemums, dahlias, peonies, rhododendron or laurel blossoms.

- Use an old-fashioned square, footed candy compote to make a Victorian nosegay centerpiece. Cluster many shaggy pompons, chrysanthemums, daisies, peonies, carnations; and border the nosegay with shiny green rhododendron leaves.

- Make a nosegay for each place, using a small rounded glass or an eggcup, with a small bunch of flowers and green leaves circled with a ruffly paper doily.

- Put a stiff bright row of geraniums in the center of the table. You could paint the pots white or wrap them prettily in gift paper or striped crepe paper.

- Put a metal or glass dish or jar inside a wicker basket and fill it with assorted garden flowers put in at random.

- Take any leafy house plant of fairly good size (depending on your table) and carefully stick poles of small bright flags in the soil.

- During the Christmas season, fill a big shallow bowl with Christmas-tree balls, perhaps with a few spikes of holly.

- Fill a dish with styrofoam snowballs and insert candy canes in the pile of snowballs—like a porcupine.

222

- In May, little baskets of flowers at each place—or a basket in the center with ribbons to each place—would be traditional.
- Sometimes the cake you plan for dessert—such as a Valentine's cake, logroll for Lincoln's Birthday, cherry-trimmed cake for Washington's Birthday—makes a centerpiece that might well be called mouth-watering!

PARTY MENUS

Here are menus and recipes for a variety of parties. Dishes marked with a star are the ones for which you'll find recipes.

Back-yard Barbecue
    barbecued hamburgers and frankfurters
    baked spaghetti casserole
    apple nut salad
    assorted relishes
    toasted rolls
    chilled watermelon   coconut meringue kisses *
    fruit jubilee *

Before-the-Dance Party
    toothpick tantalizers *
    petits fours *
    Cuban cola *

Festive Occasion Parties (Tea, Shower, Graduation, Etc.)
    grenadine-grapefruit juice cocktail *
    checkerboard, pinwheel, and rolled tea sandwiches *
    everything nice salad *
    sweetheart angel cake *
    jewel fruit punch *

223

Summer Lunch 1

    pineapple-lemon gelatin ring with choices of tuna, shrimp, or
        chicken salad and Slenderette dressing *
    toasted English muffins
    ice-cream puff with berry sauce
    iced tea   iced coffee

Summer Lunch 2

    Seventeen salad and dressing *
    hot buttered biscuits or popovers
    brownies
    ice-cream soda à la maison *

Winter Lunch 1

    tomato juice cocktail with cheese-flavored Melba toast *
    shrimp Newburg and rice
    vitality salad *
    applesauce loaf *
    hot coffee with whipped cream
    hot chocolate with whipped cream

Winter Lunch 2

    pineapple cocktail with cinnamon graham crackers
    chicken à la king   rice ring
    asparagus vinaigrette *
    royal ring ginger cake filled with lemon hard sauce *
    hot coffee   chocolate milk

Casserole Supper 1

    heavenly herbed hamburger * with mushroom sauce
    mixed vegetable salad with sour-cream dressing *

224

checkerboard cakes *
mocha milk float

Casserole Supper 2

B.B. and B.F. casserole *
cucumber or beet ring filled with chive cottage cheese
brown-and-serve rolls
cherry parfait with whipped-cream topping *
milk   coffee

Summer Brunch 1

bouillon on the rocks
showcase ham and eggs *
garden state salad *
buttered toast rounds
minted melon balls *
milk   coffee

Summer Brunch 2

bouillon on the rocks
waffles with chicken hash
celery   carrot sticks   radish roses
berry bowl
milk   coffee

Winter Brunch 1

broiled half grapefruit
hot bouillon
eggs benedict with cheese or hollandaise sauce
Mexican salad *
baked apples supreme *
maple-nut ladyfingers *
café au lait   hot chocolate

Winter Brunch 2

    hot bouillon   heated madrilene soup

    chicken livers sautéed with rice

    mixed green salad

    spiced peaches

    crumble cake *

    café au lait   hot chocolate

PARTY RECIPES

BACK-YARD BARBECUE

Coconut Meringue Kisses

In mixing bowl combine four egg whites and one-eighth tea-spoon salt. With electric mixer or rotary beater, beat until soft peaks form. Beat in, one tablespoon at a time, one cup sugar. Beat well after each addition. To every cup of meringue, fold in one-half cup of flaked coconut. Drop meringue by teaspoonfuls, one inch apart, onto greased cookie sheet and bake at 250°F. (slow oven) for one hour. Makes about four dozen kisses.

Fruit Jubilee

Combine two six-ounce cans frozen lemonade concentrate with one twelve-ounce can each pear nectar and apricot nectar and one pint apple juice. Chill. When ready to serve, add two twenty-eight-ounce bottles sparkling water and pour over ice in punch bowl. Float fresh lemon slices, each garnished with a whole clove, on the punch. Makes twenty-six four-ounce servings.

BEFORE-THE-DANCE PARTY

Toothpick Tantalizers

BACON KABOBS: Wrap stuffed green olives, tiny pickles, ham cubes, or small button mushrooms in small strips of bacon. Fasten with toothpicks and broil until bacon is crisp.

SHRIMP AND PINEAPPLE KABOBS: Lace a small chilled cooked shrimp and a cube of canned pineapple onto a toothpick. Provide cocktail sauce for dunking.

BABY FRANK KABOBS: Broil or sauté cocktail frankfurters or sausages. Spear each with a toothpick. Provide mustard sauce for dunking.

MEAT BALL KABOBS: Heat canned miniature meat balls over hot water or make tiny meat balls and brown lightly in a greased skillet. Serve with chili sauce for dunking.

APPLE-CHEESE KABOBS: Cut cheese into small cubes. Core and cut firm red eating apples into small wedges, dip in orange juice to prevent darkening. Lace a cheese square and an apple wedge onto toothpick.

CREAM CHEESE-PEANUT BALLS: Shape cream cheese into tiny balls. Roll each in finely chopped peanuts. Spear each with a toothpick and chill until serving time.

HAM AND CREAM CHEESE SQUARES: Stack three or four thin slices of ham together with softened cream cheese. Wrap in waxed paper and chill until serving time. Then cut into cubes and spear each with a toothpick.

STUFFED PICKLE ROLLS: With a vegetable parer, remove centers from dill pickles. Stuff each pickle tightly with liverwurst which has been blended with a small amount of crumbled bacon. Chill until serving time, then cut crosswise into one-half-inch slices. Spear each with a toothpick.

Petits Fours

Use one package of your favorite white or yellow cake mix. Prepare cake as package directs, using a thirteen-by-nine-by-two-inch pan. Cool cake about ten minutes, then remove from pan. When cake is cold, trim crusts and cut into small rectangles, squares, and diamonds. To ice, use a seven-minute frosting, or a packaged fluffy frosting mix. Divide prepared frosting into four equal parts and turn each into a separate bowl. Leave one white and tint each of the remaining a different color—pink, green, yellow. Ice top and sides of each of the cakes. Decorate with *dragées*, tinted sugar, flaked coconut, slivered nuts, chocolate shavings.

Cuban Cola

Pour into a tall glass one chilled six-ounce bottle cola beverage. Add one-half to one teaspoon instant coffee powder and one teaspoon lemon juice. Stir well to dissolve coffee powder. Add ice cubes and serve at once.

FESTIVE OCCASION PARTIES
(tea, shower, graduation, etc.)

Grenadine-Grapefruit Juice Cocktail

Fill cocktail glasses with crushed ice. Combine two cups chilled unsweetened grapefruit juice and one-half cup nonalcoholic grenadine; mix well. Pour over the crushed ice. Garnish each glass with a sprig of fresh mint which has been dipped in lemon juice and sprinkled lightly with granulated sugar. Yield: seven glasses.

Tea Sandwiches

ROLL-UPS: Trim crusts from slices of fresh white bread. Run a rolling pin lightly over each slice and spread each with softened cream cheese or minced chicken and egg salad. Roll up, jelly-roll fashion, and tuck a sprig of water cress in one or both ends of each roll-up. Store in refrigerator, seam side down, until serving time.

CHECKERBOARDS: Trim crusts from two slices of white bread and two slices of whole-wheat bread. Alternately stack the dark and white slices, spreading three of the slices with a blend of minced ham, finely chopped sweet pickle, and mayonnaise. Top with the fourth slice. With palm of hand, lightly press stack together. Then cut into one-half-inch slices. Using softened butter as a filling, restack slices, alternating dark and light edges. Wrap in waxed paper and chill in refrigerator for two to three hours. Just before serving, remove from refrigerator. Using sharp knife, slice into checkerboard slices, one-half inch thick.

PINWHEELS: Trim crusts from an unsliced loaf of white bread. Then cut bread into lengthwise slices, about one-fourth inch thick. Run rolling pin lightly over each slice, starting at the short end. Spread each slice with softened butter, then with egg or tuna salad. Now arrange stuffed olives in a row across the narrow end of each slice and roll up jelly-roll fashion. Wrap each roll in waxed paper or aluminum foil, twisting ends tightly. Chill two hours or more. Just before serving, cut chilled rolls into one-fourth- to one-half-inch slices.

RIBBONS: Spread a thin slice of date-nut bread with softened cream cheese. Then cover with a second slice of bread and cut into "ribbons" about one-half inch wide.

Everything Nice Salad

Place two or three crisp lettuce leaves on individual salad plates. Next, alternate orange, grapefruit, and avocado slices in a circular pattern on each bed of lettuce. (Dip avocado slices in lemon juice to prevent darkening.) Place a dollop of Lemon Cream Dressing in the center of each plate.

LEMON CREAM DRESSING: Gradually stir two tablespoons lemon juice into one-half cup sour cream. Add one-eighth teaspoon salt; blend well. Makes about two-thirds cup.

Sweetheart Angel Cake

Use one seventeen-ounce package angel food cake mix. Prepare as package directs and bake in a ten-inch tube cake pan. Cool and remove from pan. Place cake upside down on waxed paper or foil. Using a sharp knife, cut slice from top of cake, about one inch down. Lift off and set aside. Now, using a smaller knife and spoon, cut and scoop out about a one-inch-wide channel in the cut surface of the cake, leaving a one-inch-wide "wall" on both sides and a one-inch base on the bottom. Place on serving dish. Prepare filling: Beat together until it peaks three cups heavy cream, one-third cup confectioner's sugar, and a few drops red food coloring. Into about half the mixture, fold in one cup sliced fresh strawberries. Use to fill cavity. Replace top of cake and frost top and sides with the remaining cream. Decorate with fresh whole strawberries.

Jewel Fruit Punch

Combine in large pitcher four six-ounce cans frozen pineapple and orange juice concentrate, one six-ounce can frozen lemonade concentrate, and one quart water. Chill until ready to serve. Then pour over ice cubes in large punch bowl. Add three twenty-eight-ounce bottles ginger ale and one twenty-eight-ounce bottle sparkling water. Add one cup each of drained canned pineapple chunks, fresh whole strawberries, and fresh orange slices. Mix gently and serve. Makes about fifty four-ounce servings.

(or)

Make up your favorite fruit punch with a ginger-ale base. Pour over ice cubes in punch bowl, then add drained canned pineapple chunks, fresh whole strawberries, and fresh orange slices. Mix gently and serve.

SUMMER LUNCH 1

Pineapple-Lemon Gelatin Ring with Tuna, Shrimp, or Chicken Salad

Prepare three packages lemon-flavored gelatine as package directs. Pour one-fourth-inch gelatine mixture into a two-quart ring mold. Chill until firm. Meanwhile chill the remaining gelatine until the consistency of unbeaten egg whites. Next, spoon two cups well-drained crushed pineapple evenly over gelatine in mold. Spoon a small amount of the slightly thickened gelatine over the crushed pineapple and chill until firm. Then add remaining gelatine and chill until firm. When ready to serve, unmold on serving dish and fill center of mold with your favorite—tuna, shrimp, or chicken—salad. Garnish with sprigs of water cress and deviled eggs and serve with Slenderette Dressing.

> SLENDERETTE DRESSING: Combine one cup salad dressing, one-half cup skim milk, four tablespoons each ketchup and chopped sweet pickle, and two tablespoons lemon juice. Mix well and chill until ready to serve.

SUMMER LUNCH 2

SEVENTEEN Salad and Dressing

In salad bowl combine prepared salad greens (lettuce, romaine, chicory, and water cress). Add a small amount of SEVENTEEN Dressing and toss lightly. In center of salad arrange thinly sliced celery, julienne ham or tongue, thin slices of cheese, and finely chopped hard-cooked egg. Sprinkle with minced chives. Garnish with tomato wedges and serve at once with more dressing.

> SEVENTEEN DRESSING: Combine in jar with cover one-fourth cup each salad oil and water, one-half cup lemon juice, one teaspoon chili sauce, one-half teaspoon salt, one-fourth teaspoon garlic or onion powder, and one tablespoon capers. Shake well and chill. Makes about one cup.

Ice-Cream Soda à la Maison

Combine in blender one cup chilled root beer and one small scoop vanilla ice cream. Run blender until foamy. Pour into tall glass and serve at once.

WINTER LUNCH 1

Cheese-Flavored Melba Toast

Spread Melba toast with softened butter. Sprinkle each slice lightly with grated American cheese. Toast under broiler for a few minutes until cheese melts. Serve with Tomato Juice Cocktail.

Vitality Salad

In refrigerator marinate separately in French dressing, for one hour, two cups sliced tomatoes and two cups each of the following cooked vegetables: succotash, cauliflowerets, cut green beans. Line salad bowl with crisp chicory or romaine. Place four lettuce cups around center of bowl. Fill each with one of the marinated vegetables and garnish center of bowl with water cress. Serves six.

Applesauce Loaf

Use your favorite recipe for applesauce cake and bake in a long loaf pan until cake tests done. Cool on wire rack for ten minutes, then remove from pan. When cake is cold, ice top and sides with a Lemon Cream-Cheese Frosting.

WINTER LUNCH 2

Asparagus Vinaigrette

Place small bundles of chilled cooked asparagus tips in individual lettuce cups. Over each bundle arrange two or three pimiento strips and dust lightly with minced fresh basil. Spoon one to two tablespoons French dressing over each asparagus bundle. Garnish with tomato wedges.

Royal Ring Ginger Cake Filled with Lemon Hard Sauce

Use one package of your favorite gingerbread cake mix. Prepare as package directs and bake in a one-and-one-half-quart ring mold until cake tests done. Cool on wire rack for ten minutes, then invert on serving plate. When ready to serve, fill hole in center of cake with Lemon Hard Sauce which has been shaped into small balls.

LEMON HARD SAUCE: Combine in mixing bowl one-third cup butter or margarine, one cup sifted confectioner's sugar. Beat until light and fluffy. Add two teaspoons lemon juice and two teaspoons grated lemon rind; mix well. Roll into small balls and refrigerate until firm.

CASSEROLE SUPPER 1

Heavenly Herbed Hamburgers

Toss one pound ground steak with one tablespoon minced chervil or parsley, one teaspoon salt, one-fourth teaspoon pepper, and enough ice water and milk to make meat mushy. Divide meat mixture into four equal parts. Place each on a toasted bread round and gently shape each into a high swirled mound. Make impression, about one inch deep, on top of each mound and fill with ketchup. Preheat broiler at 375° F. about ten minutes. Arrange swirled mounds on broiler rack and broil about five inches away from heat until desired degree of doneness. Yield: four servings.

Mixed Vegetable Salad with Sour-Cream Dressing

Combine in large salad bowl two heads Boston lettuce, washed, dried, and torn into bite-size pieces; one green pepper, washed, seeded, and cut into thin slices; one large cucumber, peeled and cut into paper-thin slices; one Bermuda onion, peeled and cut into thin slices. In large measuring cup combine one cup sour cream, two tablespoons lemon juice, one tablespoon finely chopped chives, and salt and pepper to taste. Pour half over vegetables in bowl and toss lightly. Add more dressing if desired. Yield: four servings.

Checkerboard Cakes

Use one package each of your favorite chocolate and white cake mix. Prepare as packages direct and bake in two thirteen-by-nine-inch cake pans until cakes test done. Cool on wire racks for ten minutes and remove from pans. When thoroughly cold, trim crusts and split cakes to make two layers each. Using your favorite chocolate frosting as a filling, put a chocolate and a white layer together. Halve lengthwise, then cut each half crosswise into one-inch slices. Using more chocolate frosting, put these slices together in pairs,

234

alternating dark and light edges. Then ice top and sides of each pair with more chocolate frosting. Repeat as above for remaining layers.

CASSEROLE SUPPER 2

B.B. and B.F. Casserole

Preheat oven at 375° F. In a one-quart casserole combine one-pound can baked beans, two six-ounce jars cocktail frankfurters (reserve about one-half cup for top of casserole), two tablespoons molasses, one tablespoon prepared mustard, one-third cup pineapple juice. Mix well. Top with the reserved frankfurters. Bake, uncovered, for thirty minutes. Serves four.

Cherry Parfait with Whipped-Cream Topping

Use one package cherry-flavored gelatine. Prepare as package directs and chill until the consistency of unbeaten egg whites. Fold in one-half cup washed and pitted fresh dark-red cherries, or one-half cup maraschino cherries. Spoon into four parfait glasses. Chill until firm. When ready to serve, top with sweetened whipped cream and a plump red cherry. Yield: four servings.

SUMMER BRUNCH

Showcase Ham and Eggs

Soften one tablespoon unflavored gelatine in two tablespoons cold chicken stock for five minutes. Meanwhile heat two cups chicken stock. Add to gelatine and stir until dissolved. Chill until the consistency of unbeaten egg white. Then pour a small amount of the gelatine mixture into four individual molds. Chill until firm. Place a poached egg, yolk side down, in each mold. Pour one-fourth cup of the slightly thickened gelatine mixture over each egg. Chill until firm. Arrange thinly sliced ham or tongue over each egg. Cover with remaining gelatine mixture. Chill until firm. Unmold and garnish with water cress or parsley. Serves four.

Garden State Salad

Wash, pat dry, and break into bite-size pieces one-half head each lettuce and romaine. Wash, pat dry, and pull apart two heads Belgian endive. Wash and pat dry one cup water cress. Arrange in salad bowl along with two tomatoes, quartered; one cucumber, peeled, scored, and sliced; six radishes, sliced. Pour French dressing over salad, toss gently, and serve at once. Serves four.

Minted Melon Balls

Place a few sprigs of fresh mint and a small amount of granulated sugar in a medium-size fruit compote. With back of wooden spoon, crush mint leaves against bottom and sides of compote. Fill with chilled fresh or partially thawed frozen melon balls (watermelon, cantaloupe, honeydew). Mix gently and refrigerate until serving time. Garnish with mint leaves which have been dipped in lemon juice and dusted with sugar.

WINTER BRUNCH 1

Mexican Salad

In mixing bowl combine three cups drained canned kernel corn, one-half cup chopped green pepper, one-fourth cup chopped pimiento, two slices toast cut into small cubes. Add about one-half cup French dressing and mix gently. Line four individual salad plates with crisp lettuce leaves. Spoon one fourth the mixture on each bed of lettuce. Garnish with tomato slices. Yield: four servings.

Baked Apples Supreme

Wash and core large red cooking apples. Starting at stem end, pare top fourth of each apple. Place in shallow baking pan, stem ends up. Stuff large cavity in center of each apple with a mixture of miniature marshmallows, chopped dates and walnuts, raisins, and honey. Combine equal amounts of honey and water and spoon over apples. Bake at 350°F., spooning syrup from pan over apples often, for one half to one hour, or until apples are easily pierced with a fork.

Maple-Nut Ladyfingers

Beat heavy cream, enough sugar to sweeten, and a few drops of maple flavoring together until peaks form. Fold in finely chopped walnuts and spread generously over bottom halves of ladyfingers. Cover with top halves and serve at once.

WINTER BRUNCH 2

Crumble Cake

In mixing bowl combine one-half cup brown sugar, two table-spoons flour, one and one-half teaspoons cinnamon, two tablespoons melted butter, and two-thirds cup chopped pecans. Set aside. Using your favorite yellow cake mix, prepare batter as package directs. Turn into a thirteen-by-nine-inch cake pan. Sprinkle crumb mixture evenly over top of batter and bake until cake tests done.